IN AT THE DEEP END

THE BIRTH PANGS OF AN ICON

By Colin Brown

"The Deep is the best example I know of a brilliant idea, promoted by visionary advocates [Colin Brown and Councillor David Gemmell] fulfilling a local need through a national initiative.
Sammy's Point was a derelict eyesore in a wonderful location at the junction of two rivers. Now it's the site of one of the finest tourist attractions in the country."

Right Honourable Alan Johnson MP, Home Secretary 2009/10

"We wrote a Harvard Business School teaching case on Colin Brown and the founding of The Deep, as an excellent example of leadership and entrepreneurship in the public sector.
Brown tells this captivating story with great humor and the same passion which has led to the success of The Deep."

Amy C. Edmondson Professor of Leadership and Management Harvard, and Dr Barbara Z. Larson, Lecturer in Organisational Behavior Harvard Business School.

ISBN   978-0-9575723-0-0
PUBLISHED BY STATION PUBLISHING.
COPYRIGHT 2013 COLIN BROWN
ALL RIGHTS RESERVED.

Preface

"We need another and wiser, perhaps more mystical concept of animals.
In a world older and more complete than ours they move finished and complete.
Listening with senses we have never attained, living with voices we shall never hear.
They are not brethren, they are not underlings, they are other nations caught with ourselves in a net of life and time".

Henry Bessant

This book has been written to mark 5 million visitors to The Deep in Hull. It is based almost entirely on my recollection of events and conversations which took place, in most cases over a decade earlier. As such it is an accurate history of the project only to the same extent that a Harry Potter novel is an accurate description of the English Public School system! Any errors, omissions, unintended insults, exaggerations or indeed sacrilege are therefore entirely my own fault.

I would like to thank everyone who helped and supported our work on The Deep but particularly David Gemmell who travelled beside me on this road and who has become a trusted friend, The Deep crew, the Board and the people of Hull; I hope we have made you proud.

All profits from the sale of this book....should there be any....will be donated to Marine Conservation Charities

Colin Brown, Chief Executive

For Nicola

Contents

				Page No.
Chapter 1	Screaming at Goldfish	Spring	2000	3
Chapter 2	Hull you're welcome to it	Summer	1995	5
Chapter 3	Bring me a Dodo	Autumn	1995	11
Chapter 4	The Evolving sea	Winter	1995/1996	19
Chapter 5	The Devil and the Partners	Spring	1996	25
Chapter 6	Building support	Summer	1996	33
Chapter 7	The site, the story and the scripture	Autumn	1996	43
Chapter 8	When in doubt do nothing	Winter	1996/1997	49
Chapter 9	The Bridge and the Business Centre	Spring	1997	55
Chapter 10	The Lucky Little Devil bottles it	Summer	1997	59
Chapter 11	The Longest Day	Autumn	1997	67
Chapter 12	The Decision	Winter	1997/1998	73
Chapter 13	After the news	Spring	1998	79
Chapter 14	Portugal	Summer	1998	85
Chapter 15	Out with the old	Autumn	1998	91
Chapter 16	Camden Library	Winter	1998/1999	103
Chapter 17	HMS Sinking ship	Spring	1999	113
Chapter 18	Contract Killing	Summer	1999	119
Chapter 19	Oswald T. Hall	Autumn	1999	125
Chapter 20	California Dreaming	Winter	1999/2000	129
Chapter 21	On your marks ... get set... wait	Spring	2000	139
Chapter 22	I am seconded	Summer	2000	151
Chapter 23	Aquarists Assemble!	Autumn	2000	157
Chapter 24	The Bleak Mid-winter	Winter	2000/2001	161
Chapter 25	The Lucky Devil v The Millennium bug	Spring	2001	169
Chapter 26	The PM	Summer	2001	175
Chapter 27	Biology	Autumn	2001	181
Chapter 28	What the F*** is a Submarium?	Winter	2001/2002	185
Chapter 29	The Opening	Spring	2002	193
Chapter 30	Post-opening	Summer	2002 onwards.	198
Chapter 31	Research and Conservation	On-going		201
List of plates.				205

CHAPTER 1   **SPRING 2000**

SCREAMING AT GOLDFISH

"Many experiences perceived as coincidence were not merely due to chance but....suggested the manifestation of parallel events or circumstances. This I call Synchronicity, or meaningful coincidence."

Carl Jung

Sunday 26th March 2000 was unseasonably warm, which together with my fear was already causing tiny beads of sweat to gather at the nape of my neck. Crouching low over my small garden pond, I placed my nose close to the water, like a rather middle-aged cat and peered intently at my only goldfish cruising lazily through the pond weed. I stared at the water, reflecting for a while, my reflection stared back. Slightly receding hairline, slightly over-weight, nose more than slightly too big.

I checked that I was alone. Good! My wife was still indoors and my two teenage daughters were at that age when gardens, sunshine and mornings are all equally unattractive. Drawing a deep breath I let out a loud bellow, aiming the sound directly at Humphrey the fish. Fear gave another twist to my insides as the fish, now totally immobile, appeared dead. I tried again, this time louder, a fog-horn sounding in the clear East Yorkshire air. Still the fish showed no sign of life. I slumped down on the grass. Oh my God, I thought, I've killed Humphrey the goldfish and bankrupted the 8th biggest City in England.

The story which had led me to this conclusion had, truth be told, begun some 5 years earlier and would in time deliver a quite remarkable building. In time it would become a unique Millennium project and would change a City's image forever. In time it would become The Deep, a Visitor Attraction telling the story of the world's oceans from earliest myths to the present day. But right now and as so often during the last 5 years, that outcome seemed unlikely in the extreme. "What on earth had this job reduced me to?" I wondered, Chief Executive of a £45 million aquarium project and here I was testing the theory that the sound from an immovable fog-horn thoughtfully situated 5 metres from our equally immovable shark tank, would, as we had just been advised, stun all of our fish every time the River Humber turned a bit misty!

I rolled over on my back and closed my eyes against the sun's glare. This isn't how it's meant to be, I thought, one surreal crisis after another. Management is meant to be a science, or at least logical. All those years of studying management was meant to put me in control of events. After all, projects written up by others had always seemed to follow a linear path, why didn't mine? As I continued to wonder where I had gone wrong, I began to also wonder if the truth might be much less reassuring. Real life, at least real projects it appeared, are more Dungeons and Dragons than Dragons Den, more Willy Wonka than Alan Sugar. More luck than logic, more magic than management. If I ever get through this, I thought, I'm going to expose the myth and tell the real story of The Deep, even if no one believes it.

CHAPTER 2

SUMMER 1995

HULL, YOU'RE WELCOME TO IT!

"You may not be interested in strategy but strategy is interested in you."
Leon Trotsky

It had all begun in August 1995 when as a new Director of Leisure Services in Hull I had attended my first Tourism Sub-Committee (postcard sub-committee to its detractors). It was held, as was every Tourism Sub-Committee, in the oak panelled Victorian grandeur of Hull's Guildhall. The room was circled by rather bad portraits of previous Lord Mayors. Over the head of a large dark wooden table, a black and white photograph of the late Sir Leo Schultz looked down on the room. He was smiling and holding a cigarette 'à la Noel Coward'; below that, and showing an irony that went unnoticed, was a no smoking sign and below that in the Chair sat Councillor David Gemmell. A man in his mid-50s, David had been an Engineer and a Trade Union officer until Mrs. Thatcher had done away with the majority of both in the 80s. Now he dedicated his time and considerable energy to developing tourism in Hull; he had, it would seem, always liked a challenge. Next to The Chairman in the seat traditionally reserved for the Chief Officer sat me. I was 39, married with a shiny new Master's Degree in Business Administration and absolutely no idea of what contempt some of my new employers felt for Chief Officers in general and southern Chief Officers in particular.

It was whispered that Council members in Hull used to stand when Chief Officers entered the room but there had been a gradual erosion in the awe in which we, as a breed, were held until by now it was considered unnecessarily deferential for Councilors to stop reading their copy of the Racing Post whilst a Chief Officer is presenting a report.

The Chairman brought the meeting to what passed for order. "Welcome colleagues, before we start I'd like to introduce you to Colin Brown who's now taking responsibility for tourism matters, now that Mr. Dean has retired." There were a few pieces of friendly banter from the floor, as is the tradition in Hull. "We'll get rid of you too if you're no good" and "That's all we need, another bloody Southerner" and "Who is he then, what happened to the old fellow who used to sit there?"

I attempted a smile, this must be what is called plain talking in Yorkshire and is known as being bloody rude in the rest of the world, I thought.

The meeting began and after the preliminaries the discussion turned to the general position of tourism in Hull which, contrary to all perceived wisdom and southern prejudice (including mine!) was already an important industry and one with significant potential. For all their 'robustness' no one, certainly no officer, knew their city like these Councilors and no one could be more proud of its strengths, more frustrated by its lack of recognition or, touchingly, more blind to its weaknesses.

Hull had, has, a terrific tourism offer, a compact, historic city centre with a maritime backdrop, fabulous museums, mediaeval churches, the fish pavement tourism trail and a hundred stories to tell. Home to Wilberforce, the Bounty, Larkin, Beautiful South and the Civil war and port of departure to vampire hunters and Robinson Crusoe, Hull nevertheless seemed unable to break out of its tabloid, music hall image. Hull was, according to public perception, nothing, it was nowhere, and every media description of the city began 'Hull was once....'

Yet Hull's port had 1,000,000 visitors a year passing through, to York, Scotland and the Lakes. The question of how Hull with its northern fishing port label could emulate Bradford, Leeds and others and establish its self as a legitimate destination was the question which dominated - even tormented - the whole committee.

The meeting plodded on. Eventually the Members' frustration with life in general but with officers in particular, came to a head. "The bloody officers have got no idea what they're doing" stormed a particularly 'helpful' Councillor.

Now it's a great skill in local government to pick up what officers call "the feeling of the meeting". This is generally done by letting everyone have their say and then restating the views of the most powerful, volatile or threatening member in a way which would not sound unreasonable when quoted to the local press. Hence "Someone ought to string up the idiot who forgot to order the tea" becomes, "if I interpret the feeling of the meeting correctly, Members wish to formally minute their disappointment with the corporate catering functions quality control programme." A comment such as "The left hand doesn't know what the right hand is doing", becomes a request for a corporate working party on inter departmental communications and in this case "The bloody officers have got no idea what they're doing" becomes, "if I interpret the feeling of the meeting correctly, Members request the Director of Leisure produce, in consultation with others, a tourism strategy". They agreed, I sat back and smiled smugly. I was pleased with my intervention; I would begin to consider a first draft in the autumn, with perhaps a consultation paper by this time next year. "And yeah... by the next meeting" grunted the 'helpful' Councillor. This common stratagem played at the end of a debate was an effective Parthian shot, rendering at one fell stroke, the task almost impossible to achieve.

Committee meetings were, at that point, monthly and by the time a report had been commented upon by the Treasury, the Legal Department and the Political Correctness Police, been checked, typed, put into the correct format, talked through with the Chairman, rewritten, retyped, rechecked, printed and sent out in time to fulfill the open government legislation, officers had in reality about 48 hours between the monthly meetings to write reports. Back in my office and in desperation I turned to my secret stack of bottom drawer management books.

It is a little understood fact that management books fall into two distinct categories. These categories are not, as some mistakenly appear to believe, management practice and theory, but shelf books and drawer books.

Shelf books as the name implies, are for display purposes only and their primary role is to impress visitors. They are not to be read or referred to as this can not only confuse the reader but can damage the dust cover, thus obscuring the author's name and the long pretentious titles. Such books are always hardback and carry such titles as 'Human Resourcing and its role in Local Government' or 'Chief Executive Officers, their role in Strategic Goal Setting': price however is unimportant as these can, and indeed should, be purchased through the organisation's own budgets, apart from saving the recipient his/her own hard earned cash this has the added benefit of impressing junior staff who, so the theory goes, will process the order and hold you in high esteem for your greater knowledge and your continued passion for life-long learning and self-improvement.

The drawer book however must be purchased privately, preferably by a close relative and should be taken to the office in a brown paper bag and locked away in a drawer. These are the management books that are actually useful and carry titles such as 'How to write a C.V.' or 'A Beginner's Guide to Computing Terms' or 'Business Planning for the Hard of Learning'. It was to these books that I turned to for advice on writing the strategy.

I decided to allocate 24 of the 48 hours available to research, leaving more than enough time to actually write the strategy. My research revealed the following.

Firstly that the main difference between 'management' and 'strategic management' is about £50,000 a year. For this reason those who master its mysteries and understand its secrets guard their knowledge with a dedication that would make the Mafia look like an exercise in open government. However, in a spirit of the democratization of knowledge and in the pursuit of personal glory, I am now prepared to share these with you.

Secondly, do not be put off by the term 'strategy'. The reality is that at least nine out of ten of those who request strategies know less about what a strategy actually is than you do. When trying to understand the concept then, try replacing the word 'strategy' with the phrase 'what we should do next'. Thus "John can you write a strategy for the MD' becomes "John can you write down what we should do next for the MD.' (N.B. remember to title the document 'strategy' and not 'things we should do next' or the MD will probably spot the tactic).

The third secret is to understand that no matter how bad the strategy is, providing it has been 'sent for consultation' then no individual or group will feel able to question its quality or conclusions. It will take on an almost mystical quality, as if it had come from Mt. Sinai: indeed many now believe that the Ten Commandments would be obeyed more if Moses had been able to say, "after extensive consultation God and I have drafted the following..." This in itself would be of little help if it were not for the fourth secret, which is to actually consult widely. This is not as worrying or as democratic as may be at first feared, as only the most eager recipient will bother to read your covering letter, let alone the full document, leaving you with only minor alterations such as names misspellt and apostrophes mis`used . Always include the list of consultees, especially if they didn't reply, as they will then become the strategy's greatest supporters being unwilling to admit that they didn't bother to read it!

Next, remember to include a SWOT analysis. Simply, this lists the strengths, weaknesses, opportunities and threats inherent in the current position. This gives a pleasing structure to your list of things to do and allows you to list all the hobby horses currently being ridden as well as providing an opportunity to list dozens of complex issues in bullet point form rather than to attempt to draw out their complex interrelationships for which no one will thank you.

At this stage it can be a useful ploy to include not only all the things you know will happen anyway, thus appearing prescient in years to come, but also to include tasks or issues which you, personally, want addressing. An example might be to include under weaknesses, the lack of a clear internal focus for strategic planning issues, allowing you to build a Strategic Management Unit under your control to ensure you never have to personally write a strategy again.

Finally, spend some money on presentation. It needs to look business-like and have an inspirational title like "Forward Together" or "Building the Dream". Once the document is typeset, printed and a short foreword written by someone senior, it's game set and match.

So it was that armed with this knowledge I sat, feet on desk, considering the task before me: in 24 hours write a Tourism Strategy for Hull. I used a technique called mind mapping, which basically involves a flip chart and a pen. In the middle of the page I wrote the name of the subject (in this case Tourism in Hull), I drew a bubble around it and then noted everything that needed to be considered or included around it, starting with the major issues and working outwards. Eventually I ended up with a spider's web of a diagram showing everything that I had been trying to hold in my head on the subject, linked by connecting lines and arrows. Next I put all the issues into chapter headings and the chapter headings into a logical order, and subject to actually filling in the gaps, it was done! Leaving me over 18 hours to spare!

The conclusion, in short, was exactly what everybody already knew, that Hull would never be a traditional resort, but then who wanted to be, traditional resorts were in decline anyway, the future - so the evidence suggested - was in short breaks, urban tourism and cultural tourism and this at least we could be strong in.

The finished document listed many actions that needed to be taken, including reference to one of the more obvious but totally un-rideable hobby horses, namely the need for a single high profile attraction, capable of attracting a national and even international market. Whilst the need was obvious, the chances of success were about as great as Cleethorpes getting the Olympics. And so, suitably buried on page 26, paragraph 4 of sub-section 9 the strategy proposed such an attraction. Of course I had expected it to stay hidden on page 26 and it did…… at least until David read it.

CHAPTER 3 AUTUMN 1995

BRING ME A DODO!

"Those who have succeeded at anything and don't mention luck are kidding themselves. "
Larry King

I sat with my feet on the desk. With the strategy now written, perhaps I could finally put tourism on the back burner at least for a few weeks. I have long found the phrase 'back-burner' particularly useful as it implies that the inaction that follows is both planned and entirely appropriate. It implies a continued energy input when in reality, none is intended and it implies that the particular pot in question will be removed from the back-burner long before it boils over and leaves a nasty brown mess all over the cooker top.

It is a ploy however, which only appears to work effectively for senior management. Junior staff who try it tend to invite ripostes such as – "I'll give you back-burner, you pretentious little twerp" or "what a coincidence that's just where I've put your career". However, a back-burner job it was and I looked forward to being able to concentrate on other departmental matters, such as a looming budget crisis and a complete reorganisation caused by Hull having recently been told it was to become a unitary authority by next Spring.

My reverie didn't last long. Councillor Gemmell came into my office enthusing about his recent trip to the Natural History Museum in London. "You know our big attraction, the one in the strategy on page 26 I think it was, well, why don't we bring the Natural History Museum to Hull?" He said it as if he had just suggested we go for a beer. The man had actually read the strategy and clearly expected it to be delivered, or at least attempted. Such blatant disregard for the normal protocols of Local Government was shocking. It was one of those situations, one of those questions so ridiculous that I was stumped for an answer: quickly weighing up my next move I decided that to keep saying no to your Chairman, particularly one so animated by a new idea, was probably a bad career move whereas giving him a nice day out in London and letting the Natural History Museum say no, seemed a better option, and so it was that I found myself sitting opposite David on the London bound train on route to the Natural History Museum dreading the conversation and embarrassment that surely awaited us.

The Humber lay in one of its sleepy moods, a silver ribbon on the green blanket of East Yorkshire. Outside the train window the early morning sky was clear and bright. I removed the plastic disk on my 'disposable' British Rail coffee cup and wondered for a moment how anything with a half-life measured in ice-ages could be called disposable.

"What do we need to ask him?" I looked up, Councillor David Gemmell the Chairman of Hull's Tourism Committee was looking intently across at me. This was not a time for honesty. Here we were taking a day out in London to visit Dr Giles Clarke of the Natural History Museum, a man I had only spoken to briefly once before. Although he didn't yet know it we were about to ask him whether he would mind awfully opening another Natural History Museum in Hull.

The dreadful inevitability of the meeting played itself out in my imagination: "Dr Clarke I presume? Good of you to see us. We're from the North and we were wondering if you could see your way clear to opening another branch in Hull. Sort of a franchise, you know branch out a bit, give you a chance to get in on the bottom floor of Hull's cultural renaissance so to speak.

"How much money do we have, you ask?" "Well obviously we can't actually provide any capital you understand, but we're ready to do whatever it takes to..."

Running costs? "Well running costs would be a problem; you see we have so many other priorities what with..."

"A site, ah I know this one! Definitely in Hull we thought, but exactly where in Hull we have an open mind about, we thought perhaps near the Bowling Alley might be nice, very popular is bowling in Hull at the moment."

Do we have political support? "Oh now there we can be certain. No we don't! At least it's not unanimous yet, well not technically a majority either but that's only because we haven't mentioned it to anyone else yet, but rest assured Councillor Gemmell here thinks the idea's dead cool!"

"A Collection, what, you mean sort of dead dinosaurs and things?" " I think we've got an old whale somewhere, but let's face it you must have tons of dead things you could let us borrow, or we'll take them permanently off your hands if it saves you paperwork, it's really not a deal breaker for us."

In my imagination Dr Clarke let loose a vomit of distinctly un-academic language; you've never really been insulted until you've been insulted by someone well qualified, I find.

David must have noticed the haunted look in my now glazed eyes. "Colin", he repeated, "What should we ask him?" "Oh it's just an exploratory meeting" I explained," Let's try and not get too specific, you know keep it a bit non- committal.... oh and let's try and keep it quick!"

Yes, I thought, it would all end here and if its death was messy and embarrassing, then I only had myself to blame. According to the code of the Civil Servant, page 621 Section 12, subsection B (volume 3) I should have strangled the idea at birth, if for no other reason than to discourage an elected official from original thought, but I had not, and now I needed a lucky break.

The colour drained from the landscape as we began to near London. The monotone only accentuated by the garish colours of the ad man's art. An announcement came over the train's P.A. system was timed to perfection to coincide with the squeal of brakes. Whilst the words were inaudible, you could just make out the "This is your captain speaking" tone which trains have now adopted to try and convince us that they are not essentially 19th Century technology but high tech airplanes which, having carefully considered the option of flying, have instead opted for a ground living existence.

An hour later we stood gazing up at the Natural History Museum, its terracotta walls filled our vision and terror filled my heart. It's just like going to the dentist I thought. O.K. it's painful but at least when the good doctor has removed this particular molar we can go home and we need say no more about it: better than that, whenever this Chairman came up with some other similar scheme like invading Beverley or building life size replicas of the seven ancient wonders of the world in East Park, I would be able to say... "David, sit down, take a few deep breaths and recall our trip to London. Do you remember that feeling David? Do you remember the total humiliation, do you remember all the expense of the professional counselling I needed afterwards, do you want all that again, do you? Do you?"

We made our way to reception, turned left at the Tyrannosaurus Rex, up the stairs through an exhibition on evolution and eventually found Dr Clarke's office.

Dr Giles Clarke, Head of Exhibitions sat quietly with us in his office and listened politely as I explained the proposal and attempted to make the idea sound reasonable.

"So there you have it" I concluded. "It's just exploratory you know, just an idea."
"Well yes" Giles began, "It all sounds very interesting; clearly we can't commit ourselves but do keep in touch. Now, let me show you around, there have been lots of changes here recently, did you know we have the biggest collection of beetles in the world?"

As Giles began our tour David nudged me, "See I told you, nothing to it." Stunned I followed on. Incredibly he had interpreted Dr Clarke's politeness as an agreement, even as an endorsement and to some extend it had been. He had not said no, and in doing so he had made the idea a project. There could only be one of two explanations, either Giles must be one of life's gentlemen too polite to point out that we would have more chance of finding a pair of matching Holy Grails than getting The Natural History Museum to move to Hull, or alternatively someone, or something was watching us, helping. I began to feel that we were indeed being watched and by more than the security cameras, no it was impossible, but then this whole idea was impossible, This David Gemmell was impossible!

I now believe in flying saucers. For me the idea of beings from another planet visiting the earth, amusing themselves by scaring the crap out of small town America and then deciding that, whilst earth is a nice place to visit, they don't really want to live here, seems eminently reasonable. Indeed next to the half-baked so-called explanations we get given for such incidents, the existence of little green men sounds almost sane.

For example, I once heard an expert explain a particularly elaborate celestial truck stop by saying that it was probably no more than humans from the future who had mastered time travel!

As if that was more likely!

The point is that there comes a time where the explanation becomes more unlikely than the original mystery it set out to explain. I mention this only by way of introducing my own explanation of why this project didn't fall flat on its face on fifty different occasions. Put simply, I have begun to suspect that someone or something, created for us our own little helper, a guardian angel if you will, but a particularly lazy and malevolent one!

It was someone or something that would bring us luck when we needed it, but with just enough spitefulness to wait until we were wetting ourselves before it would decide to help.

After carefully considering the alternatives (hard work, expert advice, my own leadership skills or my Chairman's blind faith), I can see no more likely explanation for all that followed.

As Giles`s tour continued into some of the darker crypt-like recesses of the Museum my imagination again began to wander. This iconic building had stood for over a hundred years. It was like an ancient temple to a once all-powerful religion, its great entrance a gaping mouth feeding from the faith of its followers. Science, the new religion of the people, it alone would reveal the secrets of life to our gaze. In their search for knowledge the High Priests of science would sacrifice hundreds of small animals but, no matter into how many tiny pieces they cut them, the mysteries of life remained hidden.

These Scientists knew life was in there, and they knew it escaped almost as soon as they and their scalpels began looking, but they could not see it leave. And so the search slowly ground to a halt, the basement of the museum we now wandered through had filled not with dead animals but with the more acceptably named "exhibits." Here all the bits necessary to make life were laid out, here they accumulated, sat, and waited, resentful and brooding.

Somewhere in those dark dusty basements of the museum under the weight of all that building, all that history, sprang a new life, well not quite life, not the sort you could cut up, with a scalpel, nature had at least learnt that much. This was small, that much was certain, but being invisible it was difficult to be more accurate. It sounded, when it made any sound at all, of lottery balls plopping into a glass tube, it felt like adrenaline and it smelled, well faintly and inexplicably of cheap aftershave.

It was a Lucky Little Devil. Its mission was to give us just enough help to ensure that The Deep proceeded but never so much as to make it easy, or indeed to avoid arterial blockages for David and me.

The Lucky Little Devil yawned an unseen yawn, stretched and took a final look at his contract. It was headed Contract for the provision of Lucky breaks to The Deep Millennium Project and came on paper carrying the Department of Mythical Creatures logo. It explained that, like cats which are meant to have a secret name known only to other cats, so the Lucky Little Devil, it appeared, also had a secret name, so secret in fact that even he didn't know it. If he did his job well though and delivered The Deep, then it would be revealed to him, and once his secret name was known to him he would be free to do whatever it was Lucky Little Devils liked to do best, which as it happens is pretty much what we would do if we were that lucky. The Lucky Devil tucked the contract neatly into his invisible waist coat pocket. What a rip off thought the Lucky Devil. That's the Rumpelstiltskin story. But of course it wasn't as any Copyright lawyer would agree!

The nameless Lucky Devil followed us back to Dr Giles Clarke's office, just in time to apply a skilful nudge to the proceedings and with his work done he jumped down from Giles' desk, gave a little giggle to himself and followed the two of us back out into the corridor.

"This is part of our new evolution exhibition" said Dr Clarke, gesturing dismissively at a case containing two Dodos. I tugged at David's elbow and whispered "See they've got two Dodos! Two Dodos, they're not easy to get anymore." "Well if they've got two they might give us the small one." David turned; a mischievous smile twisted his mouth.

We did most of the evolution gallery in about twenty minutes before moving on through a rather disappointing gallery on life in the ocean and finally Dr Clarke's new prideand joy, the Earth Gallery. Soon it was time to go and after saying our good-byes, we turned to leave. "Giles", I called back. "Remind us how did we get here?"

"Up through evolution, gentlemen." I turned and looked at David.... Well at least he's still giving us the benefit of the doubt, I thought!

On the train ride home, the Lucky Little Devil sat quietly flicking through a book of names, trying to decide which one he would like as his reward for all the hard work ahead of him. Troy? No, too much like a character from a 1960s TV show. Asgaroth? Too pretentious. Dwain? Too Burberry.

My Chairman, on the other hand, was becoming more and more enthusiastic about his Natural History Museum until my veneer of control finally cracked, if I couldn't get anyone else to tell him the truth, I'd have to do it myself.

"David, we can't really bring an outreach of the Natural History Museum to Hull, the story is just too big, we can't tell the whole story of life on earth from the beginning of time until now. We have no collection, no site, no money and no expertise in Natural History, anyway why Hull?" I could sense I was beginning to hyperventilate, and tried to breath slowly and deeply, "Haven't we always said that part of the problem with other high profile attractions is that they're in the wrong place, look at the Leeds Armouries, that should have been in Sheffield where the steel for the weapons came from, but Sheffield already had the Centre for Popular Music which should have been in Liverpool, but Liverpool already had all those National Museums which would have been in London if it hadn't been for property prices! I was now rambling, "And anyway what's Hull's connection to Natural History. Was Darwin born just off the Hessle Road? Did Richard Leakey discover the first hominid skeleton in the Primark car park? Why Hull and why Natural History? Hull's a maritime city; it makes its living from the sea." I sensed I was beginning to froth at the mouth, and willed myself to stay calm. David was already looking shocked, how could I say such things when we had just received such unqualified support from the Natural History Museum, his eyes pleaded. I decided to let him down more gradually. "We could do a Natural History Museum of the sea. At least that would make sense in Hull and it wouldn't be so, well, impossible. We've both said how the Natural History Museums display of marine life was one of its weakest and if we could somehow make it about marine conservation, well at least we might be saying something new."

He agreed immediately and with a suspicious amount of glee, we would build a Natural History Museum of the sea. Thank God, I thought, I sat back in the train seat. "Well done.....sucker," whispered the Lucky Devil. David had of course completely out manoeuvred me, like the expert Union negotiator he was, he had asked for the stars and now had me convinced that I had done a good deal by getting him to settle for only a medium size Galaxy.

By the time the train had pulled into Hull Paragon Station the two of us had already mapped out the outline of the new exhibition. It would tell the story of how the oceans began, the creation of life, evolution, today's marine ecosystems and the threats and challenges the Oceans face. Whilst I had in mind a rather modest scale for our new enterprise David felt strongly that this new building would be iconic; this, he insisted, would be Hull's Sydney Opera House, our Eifel tower. It would be the sort of building that would appear on a stamp.

As the months went by and every aspect of the project changed and grew, these twin concepts of "story" and of an iconic building were both to remain intact and central to the vision. We did not realise it, but we had set not only an ambition for the project but a theme and a storyline. Almost uniquely amongst Millennium Projects this would not be a collection of exhibits but a linear story with a beginning a middle and an end.

Of course playing this game in our imagination had, it must be said, been fun. It had passed a few happy hours in a harmless way, harmless of course because it would never happen. David would see this eventually, I would work on him over the next few months, and he'd realise the problems …eventually. Eventually of course, life and politics being what they are, he'd go onto something else, or someone else.

As long as we kept this whole idea confidential it could be controlled. It must be kept between the two of us, that was the important thing!

CHAPTER 4   WINTER 1995/6

THE EVOLVING SEA

"Self confidence is the first requisite of all great undertakings."
Samuel Johnson

The very next morning at 10.00 am my phone rang. "Hi kid it's me, I'm on the mobile". The introduction was adequate, it was David; his voice was unmistakable, if not in tone, then certainly in volume. Known for possessing a problematic volume control, David had the sort of voice that is the result of the selective breeding of generations of men capable of making themselves heard over a force 10 Icelandic gale. "Hi Dave, where are you?" I asked, moving the receiver two inches further from my ear. "I'm at St. Andrew's Dock. I've got the Hull Daily Mail with me; we're doing a piece on bringing the Natural History Museum here". Without thinking my free hand found its way to my forehead and began a rapid massaging movement. "Can you come down?" he continued. "They want some details and to take my picture!"

That afternoon the Hull Daily Mail carried a full front-page story. Under a banner headline, Natural History Museum coming to Hull was a large picture – it was captioned "Councillor David Gemmell, Chairman of Hull City Council's Tourism Committee celebrating in front of the proposed site for Hull's newest attraction."

Now we were both committed, we had gone public. We were on the line, neck in the noose. He had provided not only a hostage to fortune, but he had also provided fortune with a full 747, aircrew and a demand to go to Cuba.

On the up side however, there was…no, on reflection, there was no upside. We had nothing, zilch, nowt, bugger all. We didn't even know who owned the site on which he had just announced we were about to build. Whoever it was, I suspected they had just raised the asking price. We had nothing and the price had just gone up! There was only one thing for it, one honourable course for someone with 20 years' public service to take; now out of this impossible position I made a decision. Who knows, with David's blind faith, my animal cunning forged through years in Local Government, and perhaps if our 'luck' held I might actually succeed, succeed that is in making our inevitable failure look like someone else's fault.

It was a challenge alright, but one I knew I was equal to. I would throw myself into the task, in the certain knowledge that local Councils are full of people who take great pleasure in stopping things happening. All I had to do was look like we meant it, and every auditor, lawyer and planner would become my unwitting assistant. This might be fun, I decided; let's see how far we can get before something, or more likely someone, realises what we are trying to do and calls time on the idea.

I have often wondered since then what thought process led him to his pre-emptive publicity strike. Whatever his reasons, this single act of outrageous confidence would change a city.

It was now December 1995 and David and I discussed the next step. Never having built such a facility before, I suggested we draft a document which would be basically a pre-feasibility study, and given the timetable I would have to write it over Christmas which, luckily, in Local Government, lasts for about a month.

The long Christmas break slowly rolled over into January. I sat at home; my appetite for festive TV and the remnants of the Christmas delicacies sated. I idly calculated that over the Christmas period I had lost approximately 10,000 brain cells, either through the effects of alcohol or the general process of ageing and under-use. What size of animal had 10,000 brain cells I wondered; a worm, a flea, ten policy officers? Logically then that meant that however many worms it would have taken to beat me at Chess in November, it would now take one less. God, I needed to think about something before I vegetated further.

I found a pen and paper and stared at its gaping whiteness. I have always found that the most important part of completing a difficult task is to start it, and so I took a deep breath and wrote 'Introduction' and began. "Title Page – The Evolving Sea" that was easy enough. From the other room Lisa my youngest, shouted "Dad, Simpson's' Christmas Special is on". I'd do the rest tomorrow, I thought. "OK I'm coming". Homer grabbed a beer from his fridge. Umm, that's a good idea. "Lisa, get your old Dad a beer please". After all I thought, when was the last time someone's life depended on beating a bunch of worms at any strategy based board game!

Next day I tried again. Whilst I had offered to produce a pre-feasibility study I wasn't exactly sure what a pre-feasibility study was, I was pretty sure, however, that I wouldn't be able to produce one given what we currently had. Still it wasn't what I called my document that counted, it was what it was intended to achieve that mattered and that was simple: to convince the readers, primarily Councillors, that the project was interesting, that it had some small potential for success, that it would address the issues that they felt were important and, most importantly, that it would cost them, if not nothing, then precious little. By the end of the morning the pre-feasibility study was written.

The Evolving Sea was to be a project based on the story of the sea and how life had evolved in it. It would be educational, image-enhancing, be housed in a quality iconic building and have significant regeneration benefits.

All revenue costs, which I estimated by multiplying the costs of our biggest museum by three, would be covered by admission fees, shop and catering income. Costs would be minimised by using capital money to reduce on going revenue costs and by establishing a charitable trust which would avoid eighty percent of its business rates bill. The Evolving Sea Centre would have no capital debts, no rates and regular income streams.

In this perfect, theoretical world, getting the capital was simpler still, Leeds Armouries, an attraction of similar scale, was reported to have cost £43 million; so we would need to raise between £40-£50 million. With a flourish of my pen I assumed, 50% would come from the Millennium Commission and 50% from European Regional Development Fund (ERDF), leaving City Vision (the Local Regeneration partnership) sponsorship or a private developer as fall back options.

The concept was perhaps the most difficult to describe; strangely not because we were unclear as to what we were aiming for -we had established that on the main East Coast line - but because of the lack of a suitable vocabulary to describe it. As a result, the Evolving Sea Centre was, and remained for years, best defined by what it wasn't.

Firstly, it wasn't to be a museum, not only because as such it would fail to achieve its objectives on income and image, nor because we had no collection (a significant drawback to any museum), but also because museums came under the Cultural Services Committee and would therefore, initiate a turf war between Culture and Tourism Committees.

Secondly, it couldn't exclusively be a visitor attraction because, as valuable as that would be for the tourism industry in Hull, it would not carry sufficient political weight. To do this, it would need to speak to the really pressing needs of the City: image, education, regeneration.

Its content would be driven by the story we were telling. The Evolving Sea Centre may well need to have some "real" exhibits if only to add that sense of wonder which no amount of fibre glass and graphics can replicate, but it would also need to be entertaining, educational, environmental and even inspirational. It was to be theatrical, interactive and induce a sense of wonder in the visitors.

I had recently returned from a family holiday to Orlando, where we had visited Sea World, Epcot, MGM Studios, and of course, Disney. I had been impressed by the conceit that real science was being carried out at the first two of these as well as the ways in which this was explained and displayed for the visitors. This was entertainment married to science, having an affair with theatre and so to all of the above we would add some real science.

But still the Evolving Sea Centre couldn't adequately be described as a museum or a science centre.

Years later, we finally resolved this issue by acknowledging that The Deep (as it was to become) was nothing but The Deep. It was unique. It wasn't to be like anything; to try and categorize it as something else was always to constrain its potential.

The details of our storyline I took from a lifetime study of BBC wildlife programmes and an average 'O' Level in biology. It was to include:

> The birth of the seas
> The creation of life
> Self-replicating DNA
> Marine Evolution
> Life leaves the sea
> Sea Shore interface/estuary life
> Environmental threats to the sea
> Plesiosaurus (Loch Ness)
> The return of the mammals

> Over fishing,
> Pollution, the future of man and his relationship with the ocean.

The completed document was all of 5 pages long.

I later discovered a very useful term for such ill-researched documents, a term which confers on them a status the rigour of thought does not deserve; they are called "Desktop Studies". Later still, I was to discover that consultants charge considerable sums for such Desktop Studies but then even later I was to discover that consultants charge considerable sums for everything! When I returned to work David and I arranged to present the Evolving Sea Project to key councillors, it was 6th February, 1996.

Armed with my hand written over-head slides I ran through the Evolving Sea Centre to a small audience of councillors and officers. The response was mixed, unconvinced rather than unsupportive, the outcome was perhaps predictable. We could progress the idea providing it didn't cost anything. We were in short being asked to make bricks without straw, mud or even a small wooden brick mould. Nevertheless, like Giles Clarke earlier, they hadn't exactly said no. They just hadn't said yes yet. This was not failure, it was merely temporary non-success! The next step would be to sell it to the officers.

In the pantheon of Local Government, planners are considered the thinkers, whereas the Economic Development guys are seen (at least by themselves) as the doers. As in any such situation, neither tended to have much time for the other, yet sadly neither could achieve much without the other's assistance. Organised with enough skill both sets of professionals were therefore capable of looking busy whilst achieving nothing at all.

To a mixed meeting of the above, David and I ran through our project, such as it was, enthusing about its job creation and regeneration potential. The planners were supportive, the Economic Development Agency guys dismissive. Where the planners saw a vision, the Economic Development Agency guys saw an hallucination, the line between one and the other is often very thin, but without partners (particularly a private sector one), the Economic development guys, perhaps rightly, had bigger fish to find homes for!

The meeting ended and my office emptied leaving David, me and our little invisible helper all feeling somewhat deflated. I had expected, indeed almost wanted, someone to tell us it couldn't be done, but nevertheless I was disappointed, I could have accepted an argument, but apathy was harder to bear.

Imperceptibly my attitude had changed. I had now begun to want this to succeed. Damn it, I'd spent my Christmas holiday on this; the least I had the right to expect was that I would be taken seriously. If anyone was going to stop us, they would now have to come up with a better reason than just that it wasn't possible!

David turned to me, even he looked down. "What now?" he asked. "We carry on" I heard myself saying. Although in truth I didn't know in which direction we were meant to go from here.

The next step, if there were ever to be one, would need a stroke of luck, but did luck want to be stroked?

CHAPTER 5   SPRING 1996

THE DEVIL AND THE PARTNERS

"Those who give early give twice. "
Native American saying

Having witnessed the meeting The Lucky Little Devil sat up and looked around my office, he decided he didn't want to be stroked by anyone present and so he uncrossed his legs and jumped down off my bookshelf. Getting his secret name was going to be tougher than he had thought. He had, truth be told, been doing little of late and needed some exercise anyway. A two-pronged attack was necessary. The first part was relatively easy for him, a few little coincidences, a newspaper left in an office and Jack Hardisty, maverick Professor of Environmental Studies at the University of Hull would see Councillor Gemmell's pre-emptive PR strike in the Hull Daily Mail.

The second would be trickier, somehow a copy of the same story would have to find its way to Edinburgh and then on to Phil Crane, the owner of Deep Sea World, Scotland's national aquarium. "I'll deal with the Jocks later" thought the politically incorrect Devil. "Let's set up the local connection first."

Professor Jack Hardisty was not the archetypal University Professor. Like all professors he was of course immensely enthusiastic about his subject, which involved collecting flow information from strategic points in and around the Humber and then modelling what would happen given different conditions, (no really, Jack got really enthusiastic about this stuff) but he also had an air of entrepreneurship which was both infectious and slightly disconcerting. He gave the impression of a man who, not only had the intelligence to be a successful University academic, but the desire to be rich, two often mutually exclusive career paths.

We first met through a mutual friend on board the Arctic Corsair, Hull's last sidewinder fishing trawler which was being refurbished by a community group. It was cold, damp and cramped even in the captain's quarters, I imagined what it would have been like to spend 3 weeks in Icelandic seas and wondered why such frightening jobs were always the most mourned when they disappeared.

The meeting had a clandestine air but the uncomfortable conditions hastened the conversation. After a brief explanation of his work, Jack got straight to the point.

"I read about you building a Natural History Museum of the Sea, the Humber Observatory is looking to relocate, it needs somewhere where all this data we're generating can be gathered and interpreted. We have already spent some £1.7 million on the infrastructure which could be used for matched funding. I think a partnership with the University could benefit both, and would give this centre some academic credibility."

I agreed. We knew that any Millennium Commission grant would have to be matched pound for pound from elsewhere and we would be able to use Jack's £1.7 m towards this target. But apart from the matched funding, we also needed to build a partnership impressive enough to convince the Council to take 'The Evolving Sea' further and the University would be ideal, providing as it would the as yet undefined scientific element.

I drove back to my office and considered the implications of the University as a partner when put alongside the Council and the Natural History Museum. There was indeed potential for this developing into a powerful cocktail. The major drawback was that they were all public sector and that left a massive question mark over the issue of commercial viability. Nearly 20 years of Thatcherism had changed Local Government more than many realise. Not only had structures changed but its confidence in its own ability to deliver had been damaged; it was as if we now always needed a grown up to help us, and I had been affected by this zeitgeist as much as anyone. We simply wouldn't be able to move forward without some entrepreneur coming forward offering to hold our hand and invest their own money and that really would take a miracle!

For the second time in as many weeks the Lucky Little Devil worked a series of coincidences with the precision of a grand master chess champion. The Hull Daily Mail story was sent to Leisure Week Magazine; Leisure Week Magazine was delivered to Deep Sea Leisure, check, Deep Sea Leisure internal post to Phil Crane, looking for a suitable site for his next project, checkmate.

As the Lucky Devil's end game approached, my phone rang and rang. I looked up. My secretary was rushing down the corridor to make me a cup of tea. God that woman was never around when I wanted her; reluctantly I picked up the phone myself, as I did so Lorraine burst back in to her adjoining office, cheeks flushed, files under one arm and with my tea in her hand and picked up her extension. "It's alright Lorraine I've got it now" I said wearily. Lorraine hung up and muttered something through clenched teeth. "Hello, Colin Brown Director of Leisure, can I help you?" "Hello my name is Phil Crane. I wrote to you a few weeks ago. I fumbled quickly through my in-tray. His letter was dated 1st April I noted....

It transpired that Phil had been born in Hedon, one of the few villages East of Hull and had seen a reference to our plans for a Natural History Museum of the Sea in a leisure magazine.

Phil explained that he had opened and still owned Deep Sea World, The National Aquarium of Scotland to the North of Edinburgh. This surprised me since not only did I not know there was a National Aquarium in Scotland, but I hadn't realised there was anything North of Edinburgh which wasn't covered in white fur or heather. Phil explained it was one of Scotland's most successful attractions and he was now looking for additional sites. The idea of a Natural History Museum of the Sea was wonderful and could he come to see me to talk about the possibility of including an aquarium in the project.

I briefed David and a week later we met with Phil and his architect from Buttress, Fuller and Alsop to discuss the idea. Phil was tall, dark, handsome, rich and fun. If only I had been better looking, taller, darker and had more money we could have been twins, I thought. He explained that his site in Scotland was successful and he was in the process of floating his company, and of looking for an East Coast site. Our project, if married to an aquarium would be perfect; he would provide the expertise and, perhaps, £5,000,000 investment. We would provide a site and grant support. Aquariums, he explained, had more repeat visits than other attractions and this would clearly assist in the long-term viability of the project.

We shook hands with Phil and his friend and they left. David and I just shook. Phil's offer had given us answers to almost all of the questions which to-date we had been aware of but had largely ignored.

We began to imagine a facility, which was basically a cloverleaf, one third University research, one third educational, interactive visitor attraction, and one third commercial aquarium. We had a private partner and we had £5,000,000. It was time to talk to the Economic Development staff again.

We re-convened our officer meeting and the change was palpable, as if someone had flicked a switch; suddenly the attitude of the Economic Development Officers changed. Now there was a real chance of inward investment, the project stopped being seen as another public museum and took on new possibilities.

Leisure is seldom understood or taken seriously in Councils. It is seen as trivial, the Department of Fun and free tickets. Now though, we had a very serious agenda, money! Kevin Marshall, one of the Economic Development Agency's key players now became engaged and his support and skill were to prove invaluable. But, already time was running out, the Millennium Commission would want a considerable amount of detail for even the first stage bid proper and we had started later than everyone else. Already we would be running to catch up.

We would need the storyline developing still further as well as the initial architect's plans, detailed construction costs, planning permissions, traffic studies and of course, a full business plan, not to mention a site on which to build it. Estimates for this work, even with Buttress Fuller and Alsop working for free varied between £30,000 and £50,000. But first things first - before we even got to this point we would need to prepare our intention-to-bid letter to the Commission. If the Commission didn't consider the idea appropriate we would not even be allowed to submit a first-stage bid.

We decided that, as part of this intention-to-bid letter, we should write an intermediate stage of study, post pre-feasibility study, but pre full feasibility study; cleverly spotting the potential confusion, we christened this the Stage 2 study! To deliver it we would need some outside help and to pay for this we would need £3,000.

With commendable prudence for rate payers' money, the Council through Pat Doyle, its leader, 'allowed' me to spend up to £1,000 of my own Department's money provided that both the University and the Private Sector also donated £1,000. It was not what I had hoped for, the money was not a great deal, but I would now have to spend valuable time trying to raise the money rather than on the project itself, and with the Millennium a reasonably fixed date, time was one commodity I couldn't get sponsored!

I would start with the University. Whilst Jack Hardisty had offered the involvement of the Humber Observatory, I was conscious that the support of the University's Vice-Chancellor, David Dilks, would be key to success and by setting me the task of getting £1,000 from him, Pat Doyle had perhaps sensed the same.

By now it was May 1996 and the University campus in Hull was at its most attractive, a series of neatly open squares bordered by red brick buildings and softened by age and Virginia creepers. It sits only a mile or so from the bustle of the City Centre yet has the feel and tranquility of the countryside. Its population, Asian, Middle Eastern, African and European, was the closest thing Hull had to a cosmopolitan one.

I waited outside Professor Dilks' office until, only a few minutes after the appointed time, a tall elegant man who I judged to be in his sixties, opened the door and offered me his hand – in my naivety I had half expected to see him in cap and gown, instead he wore a grey suit with a colourful waistcoat. "Ah Mr. Brown, sorry to keep you waiting. Have you been offered tea?" His accent spoke of garden parties, dinner parties and the Conservative Party. "You know Professor Chesters don't you?"

Sitting in an easy chair Graham Chesters looked up and smiled. "Yes, we know each other, how are you Colin?"

"Fine thanks." It was a great relief to see a friendly face in the room. I had met Graham on a number of occasions, mostly in connection with his work for City Vision, Hull's Regeneration Partnership. After the few pleasantries that no meeting in the UK seems able to start without, I described the project, such as it was. Professor Dilks listened intently, asked a few questions and then proceeded to list the flaws in the scheme. It would not attract the necessary visitors; Hull is not and never would be a serious tourist destination. The Natural History Museum's continued support would be questionable.

It was clear that this was not a man used to being argued with, particularly by someone with an accent, only a little more refined than Derek Trotter. I decided to acknowledge the wisdom of the points raised, counter them gently and promise to consider how they could be resolved if we were to proceed further.

The meeting ended after about 30 minutes; Professor Dilks asked me to provide him with the names of the Trustees of the NHM and promised to mention it to his good friend, Sir Leon Brittan, an E.U. Commissioner. I left thanking them both for their valuable time and drove back to my office.

What had I achieved? I wasn't sure; had I got my £1,000? Was the University in or out; had I simply provided an amusing anecdote for Professor Dilks' next dinner party? A week later I received a letter confirming the £1,000 grant from the University and the 'Evolving Sea' took another tentative step forward. To this day I feel sure Graham Chesters' support for the project was the key.

I now had to raise £1,000 from the private sector to help fund a study that would probably never become anything other than a study and which the public would never even see. Only days after getting the University on board, the project was in danger of stalling for the lack of support from business, not because they wouldn't support it but because of a lack of understanding by the Council on how and, more importantly, when the private sector's support could reasonably be expected.

It is extremely fashionable to talk of private/public partnerships and on the face of it they have much to offer – public sector accountability and, despite the odd blip, ethics, married to the private sector's entrepreneurial skills and capital. What has not been paid enough attention to however, are the cultural clashes that such partnerships create when each partner is not fully aware of the other's legitimate agenda.

Take a simple small scale issue such as sponsorships; it is the belief amongst most in Local Government that sponsorship is money or goods provided by the private sector because of their civic responsibility and the inherent 'goodness' of the service, event, publication etc. being sponsored. It is assumed by the Council that they and the private sector share the same objectives. Whereas sponsorship to the vast majority of businesses represents image building at best, cheap advertising at least I could offer neither and was therefore seeking the most difficult type of money to obtain: free money! It was not in effect sponsorship I was asking for, it was a donation.

Again the project rested on people and their relationships. I called Mike Killoran. Mike was the manager of the City's big indoor shopping mall; as modern shopping malls go it is not the biggest, constrained in its site as it is by being built on stilts in an old city centre dock. Its uniqueness comes from this city centre location, drawing shoppers into the other shops and leisure attractions in the city rather than the more unthinking approach of many cities which have pushed these cathedrals of consumerism on to green field sites and thereby shifted their city's centre of gravity leaving historic towns full of pound shops and loan companies.

Mike would have been a British Cavalry Officer in a previous life, not particularly because of his build; he was perhaps slight, but he had a military bearing, and he also wears a suit better than any man I know. But more than his sartorial elegance, the Cavalry Officer image comes from his habit of charging any problem head on, sabre drawn. If you wanted some 'grey suits' spurned into action, invite Mike to the meeting; if you want guile look elsewhere.

I explained the situation to Mike. "So there it is, Mike, can you help?" "How much do you need?" "Only £1,000." "Go on then, if you can pull this off it will be great for the City and Princes Quay. I'll send you a cheque."

I replaced the receiver and sat back in my mock leather junior executive swivel chair with additional lumbar support. What do you know? I'd done it; it was only the first stage but at least we hadn't fallen at the first hurdle. I was pleased. I felt we had just doubled our chances of success which I now put as high at 2%, possibly 3%.

We spent some of the £3,000 on employing Peter Middleton, a leisure consultant, to work with us. Peter, a quietly spoken workaholic was my kind of guy. He had already been involved in a number of successful Millennium bids and clearly understood the process as well as anyone could have in the circumstances.

Peter's task was to develop our idea just far enough to pass the first Millennium commission test. To do this he had to convince the Commission that our project was at least worth further investigation, and that we should be allowed to prepare a proper bid. Such permission was by no means automatic. London Zoo had just had a bid for a Terry Farrell designed aquarium turned down. The Millennium Commission, we were told, did not fund aquariums. Ours was not an aquarium we insisted, at least not just an aquarium.

We also knew that they would be concerned about the number of projects already agreed to in Yorkshire. We could hardly deny we were in Yorkshire and so we argued that we were the only East Coast project between Newcastle and Norwich.

Almost single handedly Peter pulled together enough information to achieve our objective. The closing date for the notification of our intention to bid came, and our initial application letter arrived in the Commission's London HQ with just hours to spare. Before long we received confirmation that our initial letter of application had received Millennium Commission approval; Peter, though, allowed us little time to relax. To go further, Peter informed me, we would need a quantum jump in resources. The first full stage of the bid would have to be ready by November and to achieve this we would need additional staff and we would now need money, real money!

It was about to get scary.

CHAPTER 6   **SUMMER 1996**

BUILDING SUPPORT

"Press and Politicians. A delicate relationship, too close and danger ensues; too far apart and democracy itself cannot function."
Howard Brenton.

Under a cloudless sky the heat from the City's summer was soothed by a gentle breeze from the Humber. The heat in my office however, was climbing to boiling point. Peter Middleton had been right, the project had begun to generate its own momentum and was consuming more and more of my time, not least because every new crisis required a professional background I didn't have; favours were called in, help requested and positive responses were largely forthcoming but still the crises mounted in both number and complexity.

As I learnt to juggle six balls, two more were added and each day a new deadline, and a new crisis. The Department also called like an insistent child. Humberside County Council had been dissolved on April 1st and Hull had been made a Unitary Authority. I gained responsibility for Libraries, archives and bizarrely a professional Ice Hockey team, all of which came with their own budget crisis.

More troublesome still though were the difficulties in dealing with a whole new cadre of unhappy staff and vengeful Councillors which together left me with little time to push The Evolving Sea.

I could no longer do this alone. That realisation and the undeniable truth that it was indeed so, was liberating, like an alcoholic standing up and saying "Yes, I've got a problem."

Either I would get help or the project would just run into the sand. The question was whether we had managed to generate enough public and political support over the last year or so to win us the help we needed and to allow the project to go forward. There was only one way to find out, we began with the Press.

The Hull Daily Mail is a powerful organ in the City, and although opinions vary as to exactly which bodily organ it most closely resembles, it had always given us its hearty support. To date however, we had not risked significant public money: would that support remain if we had to do so? David and I arranged to see the Editor.

We waited in the Hull Daily Mail's reception area; once more the project seemed 10 minutes away from ending. If the editor refused to support our efforts, the politicians would find it much more difficult to do so.

We needn't have worried, our luck had not yet deserted us, not only could the support of the editor and his deputy not have been stronger, but they also revealed that they were sharpening their pencils, should the City Council not have the ambition to make a major Millennium bid. This would have been an attack which would have been as unexpected to the Council as it would have been damaging. Focused for a generation on defence, defence of services, defence of social standards, defence of jobs, it had seldom been encouraged or indeed had the opportunity to go on the attack, to do something positive, even celebratory. Now it did and the local paper was looking for some vision. It helped of course that The Evolving Sea had a story based in the lives of Hull's people, but the Editor also realised that Hull had a need to make a statement, an affirmation that Hull believed in its future, even if it sometimes felt like no one else did.

To be given the support of the Press was one thing; it did not however bring one penny to the project or one extra pair of hands to help. For that we would have to go back a second time to the Council, and this time we wouldn't be asking for petty cash. We had been told to go ahead with the project only if it was at no cost to the Council but we had reached as far as was possible on that basis and we could avoid the issue no longer .The Council would be our next stop.

I walked from my office through Queen's Gardens pausing briefly to admire the carnival colours of the formal bedding. The pelargoniums, cannas and lobelia were probably two weeks from their full bloom and were if anything more attractive for the promise they still held. The Guildhall, by contrast, is not subject to the ebbs and flows of the seasons nor even, it seems, the years. Its Victorian façade holds no promise for the future, it speaks instead only of past wealth and of a power, distant and alien to so many. A sandstone slab, its windows high and imperious, looked down on me as I trotted inside to the oak-panelled lobby.

What would the City Fathers who built this have thought of our little project? Perhaps on the face of it not much, but they did understand civic pride. This Guildhall could certainly have been built for less money. It could have been built without the foaming sculpture of Britannia on her sea chariot, without the intricate teak carvings of the fruits of the land and sea, without the 365 Yorkshire roses set in plaster on the Council Chamber roof. The City Fathers would certainly have understood the benefits of bringing science to a wider audience and they would have understood the business benefits that education and science could bring, but that was a long time ago. Did such vision still exist in the cynical cost-driven 90s or had it been eroded by the years?

There were still a few minutes to go before my appointment with the Chief Executive and the Council leaders, and I sat briefly outside his room rehearsing my arguments: regeneration, education, tourism, image and a chance, - no, more than a chance -, the possibility, to bring millions of pounds of grants into the City.

A few minutes later, David arrived and we were joined by Councillor Doyle and the most senior politicians and officers in the City: we began to explain the situation. We told them that we had "passed" our first test with the Millennium Commission and we now needed to spend about £30,000 to stand a chance of succeeding in the next round. The process was, I explained, a little like poker, every time someone dropped out of the game, the stakes increased; only the winners would be able to regain their stake money.

Whilst the reaction was generally positive, there was clearly a lot of concern about how taking such a risk would play with the public. Would the City want to call or raise the stakes? The discussion continued until David played our ace by telling the meeting of our encounter with The Hull Daily Mail. The local paper would support a decision to proceed. We got our money and the Council's support - we would carry on.

With the necessary funds in place, we began to deal with the need for a project team.

By the end of the autumn we would either have spent our newly promised grant on producing a viable preliminary bid or we would fall at this second, serious hurdle. The work and complexity involved with the project had been growing exponentially now for some weeks. I had certainly received help, but no one had been dedicated to the project. I didn't have the skills needed and for once they weren't even available to me in my department. Being Director of Leisure did mean that I had over 200 staff to call on and people like my head of admin and others had done what they could to help, but there is after all only so much you can ask a Sports Development officer or a Curator of Fine Art to do before they start to search their Job Description for any mention of fish keeping! If we were going to succeed we needed a corporate response. I needed a small dedicated team with the right skills to work with me.

You would imagine that in a £22m organisation this would not be difficult. But it is. Everyone had recently suffered severe budget cuts – in my department it was 16%, in Planning it was rumoured to be 75%. I needed enthusiastic staff who wanted to make a name for themselves and yet were still young enough not to have yet realised that in Local Government making a name for yourself is not necessarily a good career move.

Two weeks later I first met what was to become known as The Home Team, Gill, Nick and Carl.

Gill was a slender, even frail 20 something; her small round spectacles under short auburn hair gave her a studious look, an impression accentuated by her hesitant speech as if she were choosing each word carefully. In the months and even years to come, Gill would prove to be invaluable, intelligent, hardworking and knowledgeable in a range of subjects including planning and funding regimes which were so labyrinthine and tedious that they would send most people into either confusion or deep sleep.

If Gill was studious, diligent, dogged, Nick by contrast was the risk taker, the deal maker; his background in the Economic Development Agency working with developers and private business would also prove invaluable. Nick was about the same age as Gill, dark with a Jack-the-lad confidence and a ready smile. In their personalities they mirrored exactly the rivalries between their departments. Unusually though, these two complemented each other in their work. Although never personal, their mutual distrust only slowly matured into mutual respect, they remained at times, I think, exasperated with each other.

I asked my own Lottery Officer, Carl Burn to join Nick and Gill. Carl had come to the Department in one of the recent reshuffles, the Direct Services Organisation, the Council's contracting arm seemed destined to go through from time to time. Carl's background, like my own, had been in sports centre management, a role which, although not exactly requiring a classics education, neither deserves its testosterone and track suit image. It does need good people skills and a willingness to turn your hand to whatever needs doing. Carl certainly brought these attributes and again, as the project developed, Carl grew into the role and worked effectively at whatever and whenever the situation demanded.

I had cleared a small room in the first floor of Leisure Services offices and furnished it with whatever furniture we could find and waited for the arrival of my new team, on which so much seemed to depend.

On Monday morning in the twenty minutes or so before my trio of eager young things joined me in this shabby little office space, I wondered about their motives. Did they already 'feel' for the project as I did, or was it just another task that being the youngest had been delegated on them from a great height? Were they coming just to go through the processes and return to their own worlds and careers as soon as possible, or were they coming wanting to achieve something?

Nick and Gill arrived together. I telephoned Carl and asked him to come down and join us and I made my by now familiar presentation on the aims of the project, the timescales and the task ahead.

I left them with a quote from Winston Churchill which I had discovered the previous week and had been looking for a chance to use. "It is not enough that we try our best" I told them. "We must succeed in what we set out to achieve." There is sometimes a thin line between leadership and lunacy; I think I left them trying to decide which side of that line I was on.

The first task for the team was to confirm just how long we had to prepare our bid. There had been talk for some months that an additional round of bidding was being planned which would have given us another six months to do the work. Instead, Carl confirmed that this was indeed going to be the final round. We now had less than 13 weeks to take an idea from an outline proposal, to a detailed, deliverable project and it was already clear that our Council grant would be insufficient and so Gill prepared an application to City Vision for some additional funds to allow us to extend Peter Middleton's commission and to carry out a range of other studies.

The project ratcheted up again; it was already showing a tendency to grow in distinct jumps not gradually as one might have expected; the arrival of the Home Team was to initiate such a step change in activity.

Meanwhile, with the public support of the Hull Daily Mail, the wider City's interest in the project was also growing. Invitations for me to speak to groups such as the Chambers of Trade, Residents' Associations and senior citizen groups began to come in. If we were to succeed we needed to win the debate in the City and we needed friends. Sometimes these friends would appear in the strangest most unexpected of places; so no request was turned down and slowly we built a bedrock of support and knowledge in the City. Far from being an unnecessary distraction to our work I found these presentations to be inspirational. The questions we were asked helped clarify our thoughts and began to help us see how our potential customers might respond. What was of concern is that all through these dozens of presentations I can't recall one comment that our plan shouldn't happen, but we received many that it wouldn't happen. We were told that if we were trying to get this done in Leeds or Sheffield, we would probably succeed but not in Hull. These people had become used to disappointment and we became more and more determined not to add to this.

We had kept in touch with Phil Crane over the months, taking what advice he offered, but now as the summer wore on, it was time to see Phil once more on his own territory and confirm his commitment and contribution and so, David, Kevin Marshall and I met at Hull Railway Station and boarded the 7.32am to Edinburgh.

The Lucky Little Devil deliberately missed the train......I'll go tomorrow, he thought.

The journey to Edinburgh was filled with optimistic talk of things that might be, the plan was to meet Phil at our hotel for dinner, to bring him up to-date, to re-establish the personal contact in preparation for a visit to Deep Sea World, Phil's aquarium in South Queensferry.

We arrived on time and checked into our hotel. After freshening up we made our way down the hotel's baronial stairway to their restaurant. Phil had just arrived and greeted us with a warm smile.

During the starter, he told us of the stresses of trying to deliver his new project, Blue Planet in Ellesmere Port and the difficulties he had experienced in accessing a

European grant. During the main course he complained of the obstacles faced by entrepreneurs in raising risk capital and of how tomorrow he would also be showing possible investors around. By the time the sweet arrived he had convinced himself that the Hull project would not generate the 30% rate of return he required.

By coffee he had in effect withdrawn from the project. David, Kevin and I retired to the bar with glum faces and indigestion. We licked our wounds and sipped our overpriced single malt whiskies. Without a private sector partner, the confidence of the City Council would crumble and the Millennium Commission would be highly suspicious of our business plan. We eventually made our sombre and sober way to bed.

That night, I had the first of many Deep-related sleepless nights. The Council had already invested money and credibility into the project and it could ill afford to lose either. Those people who thought we couldn't do it had been right, and worse of all, we had again raised expectations in the City which would never be delivered. A project born out of a desire to give Hull confidence was about to achieve exactly the opposite.

With the first of the Millennium Commission inspection visits due soon I Felt I had just two weeks to come up with a completely different yet deliverable project. By the time I did eventually fall into a troubled sleep, the warmth of the previous summer's day had turned into the damp chill of an early Scottish morning.

Next day we arose and took the local train from Edinburgh to South Queensferry.... As, it would appear, did our invisible friend. The journey which we had all expected to be short seemed to last forever. After a while we realised that this was not solely a reflection of our mood but it was in fact a very long way.

All the talk the night before about Hull not being the ideal location for such a facility seemed less relevant with every mile we travelled. City centre became suburbia, and suburbia became farmland. Finally the train stopped at an unmanned station and we followed the signs down a steep winding road until we found our way to Phil's aquarium.

It was not "in" Edinburgh at all, it was inaccessible, inconvenient and yet it was very, very busy. The morning so far had only added to our sense of grievance.

If this site and these exhibits could attract 400,000 visitors a year, why did Phil not believe Hull could get its target of just over 250,000?

At our first meeting Phil had insisted that we use the accountants Coopers and Lybrand to estimate the project's potential attendances; he had commissioned them during the planning of South Queensferry and they had been within 1% of the actual figures. Their initial work was showing an average attendance of 330,000 in Hull with a pessimistic figure of 250,000 and an optimistic of 500,000. Now that it mattered, Phil seemed willing to dismiss Cooper's figures for no reason that we could identify.

Despite our disappointment and frustration, we decided to enjoy our day out as best we could. Phil's architect gave us a tour of the facility during which we caught glimpses of Phil as he carefully shepherded his investors around. Finally we sat in the imaginatively named 'Sharks' Bite' Café with the architect. "Well what do you think?" he asked. We thought the question academic at best, insensitive at worst. "It's OK." said David breaking the silence. "I think we were looking for something more ambitious for our project, but that doesn't look like happening now."

Our architect /guide looked puzzled. "What do you mean?"

David looked forlornly into his steaming coffee. "Well, last night with Phil pulling out and all".

"You don't want to take any notice of that, he was in a mood last night, worried about today. I had a chat with him on the way home, he's still keen, take it from me."

Before we had a chance to react, Phil joined us looking flushed but exhilarated by his day's work. "Sorry guys, I had to take those suits around. What do you think?" "Marvellous!" we said in unison. We finished our coffees and agreed that we would meet again in a few weeks' time. The project was on again, this thing was proving to have more lives than a cat's home!

In Local Government in the 1990s, August was the month of the ringing phone and the empty office. Councillors had recess, committees stopped and the whole Council went into a period of torpor. Of course, great importance was still placed on ensuring an adequate level of staffing was present at all times; the official line being that this was to ensure that we continue to offer a first-class service to our residents, although I have heard it mutinously suggested that certain sections dared not risk actually closing in August in case no-one noticed their absence.

Having spent my early career running swimming pools, I had always found that August holidays had been a phenomenon that only happened to other people. To me August had always meant being at my busiest, just when all my so called support staff decided to support me by going to Tenerife for two weeks. This August would, I suspected, remind me of such summers, but with the home team now in place and with Phil Crane still on board we felt we at least stood a chance of being ready for the Millennium Commission's next big test.

We called a series of meetings of consultants who met at the Guildhall. Words and Ideas, a design company recommended by the Natural History Museum, took a break from their work on the Millennium Dome to advise us on storyline, Buttress Fuller, Alsop the architects and Coopers and Lybrand accountants as recommended by Phil Crane, met to plan the work. Each would have to deliver in turn and on time if all of the pieces were to come together by our deadline. Turning the 'August effect' to our advantage we managed to ensure that tasks were given early enough so that deadlines could be set which included their holidays.

Thus a two-week deadline for a set of drawings, which might seem unreasonable in February, seems perfectly reasonable if a four week period is given at the beginning of August. It was partly with this in mind that we called what we grandly named a Summit Meeting for the end of the summer. By the time it came we would need to be a lot clearer about what this project was and how we intended to deliver it.

CHAPTER 7   AUTUMN 1996

THE SITE, THE STORY AND THE SCRIPTURE

"Wonders in the Deep"

Psalm 107

The project had begun as an outreach of the Natural History Museum but had quickly changed to a Natural History Museum of the Sea and then to a unique combination of Museum, Aquarium and Research facility. The detailed story however took longer to develop, and would continue to do so for the next 3 years. This gestation period was important. The process of shaping and reshaping the displays and story, discarding the bad and developing the good was a process which some other Millennium projects built before us may have had insufficient time to complete.

For us the process of exhibition development really began in earnest at this point. Words and Ideas, the exhibition design consultants, made a series of storyline suggestions. Using feedback from previous projects they had been involved with, they proposed that we should develop a story which would be capable of including myths and wrecks etc. This went against the scientific ethos we had for the project and proved something of a dead end, although the remains of the Myths and legends subject matter can still be viewed today in our introduction area. They also suggested the concept of an underwater research station, an idea which was to survive for more than a year before dying off and ironically being resurrected in part as late as January 2000 as Deep Blue One, the last piece of the display jigsaw.

The underwater research centre concept involved a large central tank and atrium with air locks surrounded by a series of concentric display galleries. The aquarium formed the external environment to the Station. Set on the bottom of the ocean, windows became portholes looking out to the marine world beyond.

Amongst the individual displays suggested was a column of rock which visitors could interrogate using a computer monitor, along its length fossils from the ocean's past could be viewed through a monitor. Other exhibits included a display on the history of diving, whales and dolphins, resources from the sea and the ocean X Files, a series of office filing cabinets filled with files on the mysteries of the sea, which was, I felt a contender for the worst exhibition design award (an award I later gave to the cardboard zone at the Millennium Dome).

The whole area was to be heavily themed, appearing to be reinforced against the pressures of the deep sea, whilst individual rooms would take visitors on virtual journeys out from the 'sea base' into other parts of the world's oceans.

The 'wow' factor was to be provided by one of Phil Crane's specialities, a long underwater tunnel in the base of the building. This then, together with the 3-sided shape of the building, was to be the basis for the next stage of our bid to the Millennium Commission. Before we could proceed though we also needed a working title for the project and everyone agreed that my idea of "The Evolving Sea Centre" was probably a contender for the worst name of a project award. Words and Ideas proposed about a dozen, none of which anyone took to with any enthusiasm. Eventually we decided to come back to the name at another time. Meanwhile we would choose the least bad name on the Words and Ideas list, "The Deep".

Well, I thought, at least I can spell The Deep, even if it does sound like a Peter Benchley novel. Back at the office I thumbed through my Oxford book of quotations to see if The Deep appeared in any original thoughts that I could steal.

Amongst a list of dozens, I read the following: "Those who go down to the sea in ships and make their living amongst the great waters, these people see the power of the Lord and his wonders in The Deep" (Psalms 107 vs. 23.24)

I marked the page, slowly closed the book: the quotation seemed to apply directly to Hull, not only did we have a name but we had a Biblical prophecy... this was getting weird!

With the development of the story and of the building a final decision on a site was now well overdue. With his normal vision David Gemmell had always favoured Sammy's Point, an inaccessible brown-field site at the junction of the Rivers Hull and Humber. True, there were other sites, but they were either too small or involved developing a green-field site on the City limits. For a project aiming to draw tourists into the City and regenerating its centre, an out-of-town site was less than attractive. Sammy's Point though also had its problems.

Although owned by the Council, it had been paid for by the Housing Committee which was exploring the possibility of social housing. It was one thing to spend a few thousand pounds on developing the project; it was another to take on the most powerful Committee of the Council. I decided to leave this one to David and to my growing faith in the Luck Devil who I figured would have only a relatively limited knowledge of property development but would still be able to see that having somewhere to build our project would be a distinct advantage. True, in the multi-dimensional world he inhabited, geography wasn't such a big issue but in Hull I was pretty sure it would be.

David, who had been arguing behind the scenes for some months that Sammy's Point, was not an appropriate site for housing, decided to have another shot. He went to see the Council leader Pat Doyle. It appeared that given its thousands of empty properties and the uniquely declining house prices in Hull, the proposed housing development had fallen through. Pat suggested that Sammy's Point might indeed be an ideal location for the City's new icon building and a good use for the key regeneration site. David left before Pat could change his mind… the Lucky Little Devil smiled smugly.

The Sammy's Point site was indeed ideal, it was both city centre and dramatic. It lay at the confluence of the River Hull and Humber estuary, the roughly triangular site was bounded on its third side by the extension of the M62 which runs from Liverpool through Leeds to Hull.

By some strange European Commission logic, which ignored both the North Sea and Irish Sea, it also constitutes part of a trans-European route way from St. Petersburg to Dublin, presumably vital to the Guinness for Fabergé egg trade. As a development site however it was a fund raiser's dream. It formed part of the River Hull corridor, one of the target areas key to obtaining City Vision funds; it was part of Hull's European Regional Development Fund priority 2 area. It required flood defence work triggering Environment Agency money, and was on contaminated land, it was even next to an important archaeological site which in time may unlock Heritage Lottery money.

But could it cope with the increased traffic flows? If it couldn't we would simply not be allowed to develop it. Gill of course had been on the case for some weeks and had already commissioned studies on all the possible sites. As soon as the crucial Traffic Impact Study arrived Gill came up to my office accompanied by a large grin and an even larger report held out in front of her. Would I have to read this tome? My heart sank at the prospect. "Would you like a copy?" asked Gill as if it were some exotic chocolate for my delight and pleasure. This is always a delicate moment; say no to such an offer and a sensitive employee feels their work is undervalued, misunderstood or, dangerously that their boss is lazy - sometimes all three. Say yes and you spend the next week ploughing through lists of statistics, acronyms and jargon about as decipherable as trying to work out the Enigma code on your fingers.

Although Gill's expression led me to believe otherwise, this again was a project-stopping moment. A Traffic Impact Study which recommended strongly against our favoured site would leave us with a project which might work well in Milton Keynes but which wouldn't work in Hull. I decided to ask Gill to talk me through the report which she did at some length. It could be summarised as follows: you want to build this on Sammy's Point, fine! Again the project had come through.

On October 1st I took a report to Finance and General Purposes Committee clearing the way to get the Council's formal support for the bid.

A week later I attended a full day workshop organised by the Millennium Commission for potential bidders and was struck that every other bid seemed to be way ahead of us organisationally. They all seemed to be led by dedicated Project Managers and have teams of staff; some even had their logos decided.

Clearly the competition would be very strong.

Of course even if we were successful and received a Millennium Commission grant, the Commission could, by law, provide no more than half of the money we needed, and it was becoming increasingly clear that my original plan to obtain the rest from the ERDF had been naïve in the extreme.

I took comfort in the knowledge that at least when it came to European funding the Council had a whole section dealing with European grants so at least I wouldn't be doing the work alone................told you I was naïve!

The next day a routine meeting reviewing our progress on the European Regional Development Fund bid process showed me how wrong I was. Until now the European Social Fund had been giving little cause for concern, but at this meeting it suddenly became project-threatening.

The expectation of 50% funding from Brussels had long since been replaced with a realisation that getting any European funding at all would be difficult, the European bidding procedures and guidelines made the Millennium Commissions look like a Janet and John book in comparison. We had, it would be fair to say, focused so much on obtaining Millennium Commission funding that now we found we were behind on our work to access our matched funding. Just when we needed all of our energy to meet the Millennium Commission deadline, Europe was in danger of outflanking us. Worse still, this would not simply be a matter of working harder; the whole language of Euro funding applications seemed to me a dark art, more like alchemy than application. With the right spells and incantations, performed of course by a fully apprenticed wizard, these parchments could be transformed into pure gold. But for some reason, the Council's European Officer, the high priestess of the art, took the view that her role was to advise, not to do. I can only show you the path young Skywalker, you must tread that path alone, you could almost hear her say. This was totally unfair; it used one of my own tactics against me!

Now, to Millennium Commission deadlines we would have to add European Fund deadlines. We would have to continue to concentrate on the Millennium Commission bid; after all, that work could not be added to afterwards unless at their instigation, but now we would also have to ensure that we would meet Euro deadlines. We were fighting on two fronts, all we could do was to try and stay in the game, hold the line and pray we still had a project in November when the initial Millennium application had to be in and then hope that in the few weeks in which the pressure from them was off that we could concentrate on our European flank. At this point we also became aware that as well as competing against Magna (a Millennium project in Rotherham) for Millennium funds we were also up against them for the limited European money. Given the similarity of the two projects (they were both educational visitor attractions) and the need for the Commission to have a fair geographical spread of grants, we felt it would probably be us or Magna. We felt we had a stronger Millennium bid, but they had the stronger European bid; we hoped that it may be to our advantage that the Millennium bids were to be decided first.

David and I felt that ideally both The Deep and Magna would be successful in obtaining the grants necessary, but if Magna did fail to get a Millennium grant, it would have to withdraw its European bid, leaving us with a clearer run at the available money.

This was getting more and more like a battle every day; troops were motivated but stretched and at times it seemed fighting for their careers, if not their lives. The battalions of problems kept marching towards our guns and we kept firing; but could we hold on until November?

Whilst the wider partnership looked strong on paper, in reality none of the partners could contribute much to the work that had to be done. All that work and, worse still, the pressure fell entirely on Peter Middleton, Gill, Karl, Nick and me.

Looking to share this burden I can remember finding myself in the Assistant Chief Executive's room.

I slumped into a chair and exhausted said, "I don't think anyone understands how much there still is to do."

"No, you're right "he replied and you know what… no one cares".

He hadn't even looked up from his paperwork.

Despite all the work, when it was condensed down, this stage of the bidding process demanded no more than about 30 pages of information, and with hours to spare, Carl did the London dash and delivered Hull's bid for a Millennium Project. It was for a partnership between the University of Hull, The Natural History Museum, Deep Sea World and the City Council; it was for a 4 storey triangular visitor attraction on Sammy's Point to be called "The Deep."

The second stage of a three stage Millennium bid was complete.

It was 11th November 1996.

CHAPTER 8   WINTER 1996/7

WHEN IN DOUBT DO NOTHING

"To do nothing is sometimes a good remedy."

Hippocrates

When the ERDF application was sent off a few weeks later there was an inevitable group sigh of relief and the home team, at least in part, drifted back to their normal duties. We could not justify spending even more money until the Millennium Commission had met and decided our bid's fate.

When the news came that we had succeeded, and that The Deep had come through the second round the news galvanised the team which quickly gathered itself again for the next challenge. Until then our colleagues, the partners and even we ourselves had rather believed that we would be the brave, but ultimately unsuccessful standard bearers for Hull. Like the bugler at the Charge of the Light Brigade.

But now we had made it to the final cut and had already seen off almost 90% of the other bids which had started the process with us more than a year earlier.

Whether they liked it or not, this success tied the hands of both the Council and the University. Neither could now be seen to lose confidence and pull out. Whilst this made it easier to obtain the next tranche of development money from City Vision and the City Council, it also massively increased the pressure on us to succeed. We had got them into this, and whilst we would receive our next ration of resources, it felt clear that we would both be left high and dry if in a few months' time all we had to show for the investment was a 'Dear John' letter from the Commission.

Once more the project moved up a gear and once more we faced a minefield of technical problems to be traversed.

We had been able to do little for the last few months whilst we waited to know if we had made it through the latest hurdle and as a result we now had only about 6 months to take the 30 pages of text so far assembled and turn it into a viable business. All the problems we had been able to gloss over in the last iteration now needed firm answers. More through osmosis than anything more formal the project team now seemed to include Kevin Marshall from Economic Development and a young accountant sent to be the Treasurer's representative, Neil Porteus.

Neil sort of drifted into the team, which not unreasonably initially viewed him with some suspicion.

Within a few weeks though he had become an indispensable member of the team, not least because he was good at all the bits I wasn't and the fact that he liked to party more than is natural for an accountant!

In the years that followed he would have as big an impact on the project as anyone.

This expanding team quickly settled into a routine of meetings, problem identification and resolution and I soon learnt that my most valuable contribution to these meetings was silence.

At the heart of most of the problems we faced was money. The amount we thought we could get from the European Regional development fund (ERDF) had fallen sharply, whilst Phil Crane's £5,000,000 had, it was beginning to transpire, been more of an aspiration than a promise. We had instead begun to look to other sources to make up the gap. These included English Partnerships and Yorkshire Forward, as well as a range of smaller grants and sponsorships, notably the Garfield Weston Trust. I soon discovered that it was one thing to know that funds were available from such organisations and another to have something that they would fund. One would fund flood defences but not site clearance another would fund education but not the fish tanks and yet another would fund anything as long as it was spent before some arbitrary date in the future.

As these and other problems presented themselves, planning, access, transport, legal, etc., I would sit at the table convinced that each new difficulty would be the one that would ensure our delicate paper embryo would be still born, and attempting to suggest inappropriate or overly simplistic solutions. As the team navigated the minefield, an amateur like me jumping around on a mental pogo stick was probably less than useful. With a department still to run, I decided to confine my contributions to being chief worrier and to provide encouragement and fresh oxygen from time to time by opening the door to the feted project team room and asking useful questions such as, "Everything going well, is it?" and "Would anyone like a coffee?"

We also decided that, due to his position as Chairman, and his larger bulk (which necessitated the door being opened slightly wider), both encouragement and oxygen levels were increased further when David joined me on such missions.

"Everything OK?" I asked on one such occasion, in a tone which incidentally was not necessarily demanding of a reply.

The project had by now outgrown its initial home with me in Ferensway and had established a new base at the Guildhall, the space which confronted me was filled with all the paraphernalia of a crisis control room, which in a way was exactly what it was. Flip charts covered the walls; each carried their own impenetrable code of arrows, circles, tables of figures and acronyms. Most concerning was the seemingly endless sheets entitled 'Things to do'.

Peter Middleton whose contract had been extended still further rose from his place at the centre of a huddle. "Could I have a word?" Peter led David and me out of the doorway by the elbows, and into the reception area beyond. He had the manner of a doctor about to impart some bad news. "We have a couple of problems." His words were hushed, almost conspiratorial. "We appear to be about £5 million short of our target; do you think the Council would help?" Peter turned to David as he spoke. His ebullient mood of only a minute earlier had evaporated. "No, there's just no chance. The Council doesn't have £5 million", expressing the political reality of the situation even if not the entirely accurate financial position. Peter paused for a second. "Then I don't think we can justify spending the sort of money we will need to, if we are to go the whole way. Unless we can show the Commission that we have a reasonable chance of closing the funding gap, the bid isn't going to succeed, it's just too competitive."

"What was the other problem?" I asked, curious to know what else besides total failure, could be bothering Peter. "Well we've been looking again at some of the assumptions in the business plan, and I'm afraid it just doesn't stack up at present. Unless we can get the Council to underwrite the operating costs or find another source of income from somewhere, both Europe and the Commission will drive a coach and horses through the detailed bid."

Peter could no doubt see by my fixed smile and David's slack jaw that a solution to neither problem laid here. He turned away. "We'll see what we can do," he said wearily and re-entered the project room. For probably the only time ever on the project, it was David, not I, who looked crestfallen at such a setback.

"That's it then, it's over, the Council can't find £5 million and even if it did, it won't underwrite something it knows is going to lose money and I wouldn't ask them." His shoulders dropped, his bearded chin rested wearily on his chest as we made our way along the echoing Guildhall corridor.

"Not necessarily" I said, surprising myself at my optimism. "You heard him; they're still working on it. We might have to look again at the Business Plan or increase our sponsorship targets but we've been through worse." Before he could enquire as to exactly when we had been in a worse position I continued. "Anyway, the thing is right now we can't do anything, stopping now wouldn't save anyone a penny. We're committed to paying the consultants' fees for the next few weeks; it only becomes a problem once this current phase is over. If we've still got a problem then, well yes, we would have to call it a day."

Perhaps my more upbeat reaction was hormonal, perhaps the Luck Devil had spiked my tea or perhaps it was a recognition that such an end would not fall into the personally attributable to Brown category. I like to think though that my comfort came from feeling that I had at least in my own mind, made a decision. After carefully but quickly weighing up the evidence I had decided not to do anything, whereas David had merely decided nothing could be done!

One of the few lessons I have learnt over the years is that sometimes a decision not to make a decision is the best thing a manager can do. Most projects and almost all organisations are over managed with too many bosses confusing interference with being pro-active and input with being effective. The corporate world, I have concluded, needs fewer managers with fewer pogo sticks.

By now the summer heat was a distant if fond memory, the floral bedding displays had long since been torn up and a light drizzle washed the city. Whilst the weather began to cool, so did our prospects. Not only did we still have our £5m gap and a business plan with a hole the size of the Greek national debt, but now Phil Crane was once more questioning his own role in the project. He had begun to see that his own ability to make money from the project was not as straightforward as he had hoped. Phil had always seen his role, not only as adviser but also as the project's eventual operator. Whilst neither the Council nor the University had any wish to add aquarium operations to their corporate CVs, they, on the other hand, had to go through a genuine competitive process as public money was involved. Phil perhaps understandably began to resent a potential interview process and saw this as indicative of the culture that he would have to manage under.

Nevertheless, if the bid were to progress to the next stage, the Council and City Vision, the two major funders of the feasibility study costs to date, would need to find even more money and accept the risk that, it we failed, then it would all have been wasted. In a repeat of Pat Doyle's earlier insistence that we raise at least some of the money from the private sector, heavy hints were given that we needed to get some of the costs of this next phase from Phil Crane at Deep Sea World.

Whereas I had always had a good relationship with Phil, the project had moved on and other players were emerging both from within the Council and the University some of whom seemed to come with their own different and dangerous agendas.

Whilst I had been confident from the outset that there would be an army of individuals who would come forward to stop the project, (indeed originally I had counted on it!) I had not expected them to arrive so late! Now that we were fully committed to seeing The Deep built, a squadron of individuals arrived and applied their not inconsiderable talents for time wasting and negativity to the Project. They were a burden we could have done without.

It was a bit like relying on your second to talk you out of a somewhat hasty duel only to have him turn up late and to try and take your pistol away just as the other guy was taking aim.

However, they had arrived too late. By now we had built a base of public and political support which was difficult to stop. The Deep had momentum. It seemed to be able to look after itself, it infected people with enthusiasm and before long even the most cynical individuals would often become reluctant converts.

Of course the partnership which underpinned the project and which continued to give it the credibility to withstand such attacks was still in reality as delicate as a 14 year olds ego.

David and I once more took the train to Edinburgh with a mission to save the project. We had to convince Phil that the nay-sayers had not grasped the initiative, and that he should not only stick with the project but that he should also now put some cash on the table.

Despite the reservations of his accountants, Phil agreed to put £16,000 into the next stage feasibility study on the understanding that it would be refunded if, for whatever reason, Deep Sea World were not to be involved in the operational phase.

As useful as Phil's support would be in convincing the politicians to proceed, it would all be to no avail if we could not resolve the seemingly fatal combination of a capital funding gap and a business plan which continued to look shaky.

Coopers and Lybrand's earlier review of our project had provided 3 different scenarios. The most pessimistic of which estimated that we would get only 267,462 customers a year with an average estimate of around 300,000 and an optimistic figure of close on 500,000.

Using the average figure the business plan worked, but was fragile leaving little or nothing to cover reinvestment or for the unexpected. It was clear it would be unlikely to survive the scrutiny of the Millennium Commission.

As winter dragged on, we were forced to show a relentlessly optimistic face to the world; we knew that the project now sat on a knife edge and our confidence, or at least the appearance of confidence, was all that stood between possible success and a leaking away of support that would quickly have turned into a torrent. We needed something to change the basic economics of the business plan and we needed it within a matter of weeks.

CHAPTER 9 SPRING 1997

THE BRIDGE AND THE BUSINESS CENTRE

"If you don't risk anything, you risk even more."
Erica Jong

It was one thing for The Lucky Little Devil to introduce us to the right person at the right time; it was another for him to rewrite a business plan which showed a £5,000,000 funding gap and which clearly failed to cover its long-term running costs. Of course we could always have fiddled the figures! We could have chosen not to use the average figures but to use the more optimistic ones. We could have had different accountants run the calculations again, or assume unrealistic operating costs. We would after all not be the first such project to put a positive spin on its plan to ease it through the next hurdle.

In all truthfulness though it never occurred to us to do so, not out of any overabundance of honesty but simply that we couldn't see the point in building The Deep if it couldn't survive. Neither David nor I wanted a white elephant slowly bleeding to death in the centre of the City.

The Deep would either work or it wouldn't, surely it was better to find out before we started pouring concrete than after. Ideally we were trying to make The Deep stack up at below the most pessimistic projections we had, but we were a long way from that possibility.

There was no denying it, The Lucky Little Devil would have to pull out a personal best to get us out of this one.

The answer was eventually to come from Kevin Marshall of the Council's Economic Development Agency. His idea was to build a new Business Centre on The Deep site using Yorkshire Forward, European and Lottery funding. Once built the centre would let its space to small businesses in related fields, i.e. environment, maritime, knowledge-based industries and generate perhaps as much as £250,000 a year in income as well as creating a whole range of economic outputs which would in turn help trigger other grants closing the £5,000,000 gap.

We ran the figures. The Deep Business Centre would indeed help close the funding gap and cut the visitor attraction's break-even figure by a crucial 50,000 visits a year, meaning that we now had a project that would break even with attendances at almost 5% below the most pessimistic estimates we had. It would create hundreds of quality jobs and as such would bring a whole new political drive to the project. Whilst it seemed a strange quirk of public funding that you released more money by spending more, it worked and we learnt that sometimes spending money can be the best way of saving it.

With Phil's modest financial support now in place and with the addition of the Business Centre income stream, the City's Policy Committee agreed to fund its share of the next stage of the project's development, as did City Vision and again the project leapt forward. There was still a mountain of work to be done and again little of it was my specialism. The home team of Gill, Nick and Carl, again ably led by Peter Middleton, regularly worked 12 and 13 hour days and by July 1997 the full bid was ready. It described in much more detail than previously a project which now incorporated a visitor attraction, a new foot-bridge across the River Hull, a marine technopole or Business Centre and a variety of environmental improvements around the site.

The visitor attraction, developed by Buttress Fuller, Alsop & Williams was a four storey building with three curved sides, a bit like an overinflated triangle, the Architects named it a Hullette. It had a viewing platform on the top floor and gently inward sloping sides. It contained a main tank, herring tank, a coral reef tank, touch pools and displays on the mysteries of the ocean, a library and study centre, a situations room, an area reminiscent of a Second World War operators' room and displays on whales and dolphins, a walk through tunnel and, of course, a café and shop and which would now break even at a very realistic level of usage.

The Bridge would have to be a swing bridge to ensure that the river could continue as a working river and would, we discovered, be in almost exactly the same position as a previous river crossing known as the Ha'penny Bridge.

Public consultation continued to be important, both in building and underpinning our support within the City and in developing our relationship with the Millennium Commission. So we embarked on a further series of simple consultation exercises. We stood in local shopping centres; we spoke to community groups, senior citizen clubs and anyone else that would listen.

In all the church halls and community centres in which we spoke we found the same wary enthusiasm from the public.

Most people thought it sounded great, they wished us luck, many offered us ideas and suggestions but still few really believed we could do it.

For perhaps the first time though I wasn't one of them. The addition of the Business Centre had finally given us a real, if still small, shot at success.

When completed, the draft bid documents stood over half a metre high, and would need to be proof-read, agreed by the partners, printed and copied; even given a fast track through the decision-making systems and goodwill this would take some days, probably weeks. For prudence we again decided to set our deadline for a week before the actual deadline. By then we would aim to have the facts gathered, the arguments mustered and the final version printed.

Whilst the technical inputs, outline planning permission, business plan and Stage C architect's plans were all being dealt with by the home team, David and I were tasked with trying to move the various partners to an agreement to sign the bid. All big organisations are inherently conservative and in the case of a Council and a University this is probably rightly so, neither would leave any question unasked, or any problem unresolved if they were to sign off the bid. Of course, whilst the new improved business plan had greatly reduced the financial risks for the project, they had not completely disappeared, and so one big question continued to haunt the bid – who would carry the risk?

It was a question that had been there from my first presentation on the Evolving Sea Centre, from the first moment David had come into my office that day in November 1995, and it was still there. To confront the issue prematurely would have killed the project, but to leave it too late would risk our credibility and our chances of winning a Millennium grant.

Eventually the pieces began to come together, the Council would not unconditionally underwrite the project, but we managed to put together a plan which would, if needed, reduce the break-even figure to a position where the Council could sign a partial underwrite. It was the best we could get and better, we thought, than most of the other competing projects would have. We had in effect taken the most pessimistic figures produced by Coopers and Lybrand and shown that we could now operate The Deep at attendance figures 10% below these. It would have to do.

We packed up the six copies of the documents in their presentation boxes, each with the inscription which we thought spoke to the heart of the project and to Hull and which I had stumbled upon all those months ago:

> "Those who go down to the sea in ships and make their living amongst the great waters, these people see the power of the Lord and his wonders in… The Deep."

I was pleased with the team's work. The next time that we heard from the Commission it would be with the result, there was little else I could do now but wait.

It still felt as if few people in the Council were interested in what we had done, but that was understandable as individuals continued to struggle with their day to day priorities, and in any event it would, I still thought, probably always be academic. Still, I would have liked an opportunity to have shown my bosses what we had spent their money on, to make them care as much as I now did; at least I thought that might divert the odium when the project was turned down.

My bosses are always there when I fail, it may simply be bad luck, it may be their special Local Government training, but personally I prefer to blame fate. Fate, who insists that if I'm in the same room as my boss I will suddenly and unexpectedly appear to display the IQ and verbal reasoning skills of a 'speak your weight' machine. Fate was soon to get another chance.

CHAPTER 10   SUMMER 1997

THE LUCKY LITTLE DEVIL BOTTLES IT

"Blame someone else and get on with your life."

Alan Woods

I looked around my newly decorated office. I was quite pleased with my choice of wallpaper, given that the options provided by the Council's decorators all appear to have come from a 1970's catalogue, and wondered for a moment if there was a manufacturer somewhere who specialised in municipal wallpapers – the Town Hall Collection featuring such classic designs as Town Clerk serenade, Moonlight Mayoralty or Public Works Sub-Committee paisley!

The furnishings, however, left a lot to be desired. A motley collection of odd chairs, some with arms hanging loosely down like broken limbs, others with fabric worn thin by hours of fidgety buttocks, gathered around a dark brown Formica table, apparently chosen specifically to embarrass. It was just too big for the room so that either attention was drawn to the fact that you were too fat to sit behind it, or should you still be thin enough to attempt the manoeuvre you would inevitably tear your clothes on its sharpened corners.

Still, this furniture too had its use; negotiations with Unions for example can be made more difficult by the juxtaposition of remarks like budget crisis and downsizing with 'designer furniture' and 'walnut veneer'. I had thought about changing it but no matter how hard I tried it never seemed to be a right time to buy new desks and chairs. The thing which really amazed me was that others in the organisation appeared to have mastered the technique years ago as their Jasper Conran styled rooms testified; I comforted myself that this skill at least was not one which came with rank. Chief Officers would often sit behind trestle tables whilst assistant purchasing managers or supplies officers rested their feet on antique oak desks reputed to have come from the Mayflower! I felt that I had missed an important point here, something to do with purchasing, when my phone rang.

"Lecky for you." "Thanks, Lorraine put him through".

59

Lecky (it's still very competitive) Waterhouse was our project officer at the Millennium Commission and an important bottom to be kissed. Still this had always been a particular strength of mine, although I say so myself.

"Lecky, good to hear from you, how's it going, did you have a nice weekend?" "Yes" he said coldly. "Well, you know we're still massively overbid, this being the last round, so some of the Commissioners are visiting projects to try and weed out any weak ones. It's only sensible really because it will avoid bidders in any more unnecessary work and expense. Sir John Hall has been allocated to look at bids in your area."

"Yes that sounds very wise" I said with my mouth. The bastards I thought with my brain. They've introduced another bloody hurdle; I've just told everyone we're through to the final phase and now we're back in the semis again.

"We need to arrange a convenient date" said Lecky.

"OK." I thumbed through my diary, trying to give myself as much preparation time as possible. "I'm free on the 26th, 27th, or 31st."

"Sir John and I will arrive on the 11th"

"Excellent" I replied.

"The 11th it is then."

"And we will want you to recommend a good hotel. He'll need to meet the Leader of the Council, the Chief Executive and representatives from the University and Natural History Museum and of course, yourself. Sir John will want a formal presentation, say about 20 minutes and then he'll ask questions."

"Any particular areas he might be interested in, Lecky?" I asked.

Lecky heard the question but apparently not the plea for some inside information it contained.

"He's not interested in the detail, he leaves that to others. He'll want to be told the vision. He will want to know the whole team is behind it."

I tried again. "What sort of presentation do you think might be appropriate?"

"Well, he's used to dealing with big projects; he'll expect something professional and don't forget it's still very competitive, particularly in your area. Have I already mentioned that? Never mind, see you on the 11th." Lecky hung up. "Bye" I whispered to the dialling tone and thanks a lot!

I considered the position carefully. Was this a problem or an opportunity? After all, if I played this right I might finally get some credit for all the hard work I had made the team do. Sir John Hall was coming to Hull but, more to the point, Councillor Pat Doyle, the Council Leader, would have to be there, as would the Chief Executive. Finally, I would have a captive audience!

Experienced managers will all take great pride in the assertion that they take problems and turn them into opportunities. This process is not in reality as praiseworthy as it sounds.

To illustrate: the manager will ask," Is this a problem?" If the answer is yes, then the next question is: is it a problem that you will get blamed for? It is important not to make the mistake of phrasing this question "Is it my fault?" as these are often completely unrelated issues. If the answer is that you will not get blamed, then ask yourself if you owe the potential 'blamee' a favour or alternatively can he/she be useful in the future? If they can then the problem becomes an opportunity. Simply offer to resolve the problem for them, making them indebted to you. If you don't know the person whose fault it is or if you don't need a favour from them then sit back and enjoy the ride, simply make others aware of the problem with embellishments as appropriate and savour the resulting bloodletting. Again the problem has become an opportunity for some not so innocent fun!

Unfortunately due to life being somewhat shitty, as well as the fact that others will be exercising the same strategy against you, there will be problems for which you will get blamed. These are more tricky, but, if it's a problem you can solve, then you may unfortunately need to do some real work to do so. Let your boss know you had a problem but you solved it; abracadabra the problem becomes an opportunity to look proactive.

Finally though there are those bladder-tightening problems which you know you are going to get blamed for and which you cannot solve. If it's not a serious problem, it might be an opportunity for a short holiday or to blame your workload and ask for an assistant. Finally if all else fails, it becomes what is euphemistically known as a 'career opportunity'. Hence no matter what the problem, it can become an opportunity! Sir John's visit was a problem I could solve, hence an opportunity to show off.

It was June 1997; the days that followed Lecky's phone call were hectic, bordering on panic. I knew beyond any doubt, beyond any logic, that fate awaited its chance to turn my moment of triumph into disaster, to bite me on the bum and through clenched teeth wheeze, "thought you were clever didn't you, you actually thought I was going to let you build this thing and what's more you thought I would allow your bosses to see you doing well. Get real, brother; this is Fate you're dealing with here, not some poncey Luck Devil!"

Like a lightweight boxer up against an opponent with a legendary knockout punch, I knew I could not allow Fate to land a single blow. I would plan, prepare and rehearse; I would go through every eventuality. What if the projector didn't work? I would use two! What if I forgot to mention a key point? I would learn my speech, all 30 minutes of it, by heart – I would leave nothing to chance.

Sir John Hall would arrive at the Marina Hotel at 21.30 hours on the 10th. At precisely 19.00 hours I visited the hotel, checked that the presentation boards on the project were clearly displayed in the foyer, and checked the equipment was set up and working in the function room we had hired for the occasion. I ran through the presentation again with a colleague working the equipment. I double checked the rest of the arrangements. We had agreed with the Commission that at 8.30am on the 11th, Sir John and his entourage would board the harbour master's yacht. He would go through the locks into the Humber to view the proposed site of The Deep from the river; river traffic had been cancelled until after the visit. On his return the presentation would commence, everyone had confirmed they were coming, coffee had been booked, pens, writing pads and carafes of fresh water set out neatly.

The room was arranged with a lectern at one end, the microphone worked well, but it was a modest room and if it failed, I knew I could make my voice carry. To each side of the lectern stood a projector screen, onto each was trained a computer operated PowerPoint projector. Video clips, virtual reality fly through, graphics, text slides and specially commissioned marine wildlife slides were on disc and for safety's sake also stored on hard drive.

I stood at the lectern alone, grasping it, eyes closed like a minister searching for divine inspiration. Was I ready for the morning? Had I thought of everything? Yes, I had hardly worked on anything else for two weeks. The script was, though I say so myself, inspirational. It was to begin with sepia pictures of Old Hull, fisher folk hard but proud, trawlers ploughing through Arctic tempests, ARP wardens dragging survivors from the rubble of a blitzed city, whilst Labi Siffre sang 'Something inside so Strong', an anthem of a people struggling against an unjust world, then a dark voice rings out "For a thousand years Hull has made its living from the sea, now as a new Millennium approaches" etc. etc.

The song modulates and the images change, a new Hull, a City learning, growing, modern, European and succeeding. The voice fades. The Deep is put into context, 'a new hope for the City', 'environmentally sound', 'educational', an icon etc. Then as Labi fades, the lights come up and I begin my speech, all eyes turn my way. I know this bit so well, I can deliver it and make eye contact; heck, I could probably juggle as well and not miss a word. I was ready, this time Fate would just have to lump it.

Somewhere in a seedy corner of a Hull nightclub and on a different plane of existence, Fate finally caught up with our Lucky Little Devil. "I've been looking for you, dick-head" said Fate pointing a bony finger at Lucky. "I'm only going to say this once, right - keep out of my way on this presentation thing or you might find you're not as lucky as you think!"

The Lucky Little Devil is not known for his courage under intimidation (that's the courage under intimidation elf). "Hell no man, you just say the word, I can find better things to do, no sweat, guy. Really - he's all yours." "Good, only I've been working on this guy for years, he always looks a prat in front of his bosses, oh and women of course", he added. "I mean it's what he does best, trust me."

Back at the hotel I gently closed the door on the conference room; this time I thought it's really going to work.

My alarm went off at 6.00 am; my back-up alarm went off at five past. I didn't need to wake up before 7.00 am. I dressed; best suit, silk tie, cuff links, shoes newly polished. I felt like a medieval knight dressing for battle. Management authors have always missed the point about power-dressing, dressing for success, casual Fridays etc. Dress is not important because of how others to see you, but how it makes you feel about yourself. I looked at myself one more time; I looked good and I felt good.

The car, recently serviced and refuelled, started first time and I arrived at the Moat House Hotel alarmingly early. Sir John would only recently have left for his relaxing trip up the river.

Lecky found me checking the equipment again. "Ah Colin, Sir John has decided he doesn't want to go on a boat so we've cancelled that bit of the day, ok?" "Yep, sure, no problem" I said. As Lecky turned I thought I felt the hot breath of fate on my cheeks.

Over the next hour or so the rest of the panel arrived, Councillors Doyle and Gemmell, the Chief Executive, Dr Clarke from the Natural History Museum. We sat making polite, if stilted, conversation, like applicants before a big job interview which I suppose is exactly what we were.

Suddenly the door to the conference room burst open. Sir John Hall gave us a gruff greeting and, without being directed, sat at the head of the table. His two Millennium Commission minders flanked him on either side, looking even more in awe of him than we were. I took my place at the lectern. Sir John's eyes quickly took in the scene, twin projectors, speakers, microphones. "Before you start" he said, "I haven't got time for any presentations; I just want to ask you all a few questions."

My mind raced. "Yes but we hope we can cover a lot of ground by a quick..." "No presentations" he repeated, this time with an insistence which indicated he would not repeat the request a third time. I sat down again, deflated.

After this initial disaster, the interview went surprisingly well. It helped that Councillor Doyle was not only an extremely astute and intelligent man but his role as Chair of City Vision had given him an authority even greater than that given to him by the Council. Giles Clarke gave fulsome and again articulate support as did the others.

For my part, I found myself slipping in and out of my prepared text, often in response to the most inappropriate question. Nevertheless, as a team we looked cohesive and we were not floored by any question.

As the morning wore on, Sir John began to thaw. Finally he said "This is a big bid you know, I have to be very sure before I recommend a grant the size of this one, and it's what, nearly £18 million."

"Come on" I ventured, "You can't get a decent striker now for £18 million." Newcastle United, Sir John's Football team had just bought Alan Shearer for about this figure and were going well in the league. At the reference to his beloved club, Sir John relaxed further and we all had a very enjoyable and entertaining quarter of an hour before his car arrived to whisk him to his next victim, I mean next appointment!

Fate might have managed to land a nasty left hook on me, but The Deep, at least, was still standing.

Within a matter of days we heard that we had passed this hurdle as well, and it was now only a question of responding to requests from the Millennium Commission for clarification or additional information. With each day that went by we began to believe our chances improved. We had not received any request which we could not answer and surely if a fundamental weakness remained in our bid the Commission would have brought it to our attention by now.

One by one, we began our summer vacations….. all except Fate who thought he would give it one more go!

CHAPTER 11　　　　　　　　　　　　　　AUTUMN 1997

THE LONGEST DAY

"Rumour travels faster but it don't stay put as long as the truth."
Will Rogers.

The Lucky Devil packed his holiday requisites into his carrier bag, checked that his passport and pesetas were safe and set off on his 18-30's holiday to Ibiza.

It wasn't that he particularly liked clubbing, but it was the one holiday where everyone was getting lucky anyway and he could relax in peace. Flying was also a pleasure for the Lucky Devil as without the fear of crashing which the rest of us carry on board with our duty free, he was free to enjoy the views, the fact that as a supernatural being he didn't need to eat the airline food, only added to his joy.

He was pleased with his work on the project, he figured he was due a holiday and even considering the motley bunch of humans he had to work with, he felt they could cope without him for 2 weeks.

He sat in First Class, sipped his complimentary glass of champagne which being complimentary, effervesced at him over his good looks and charm. "Your mission, Lucky Little Devil" he whispered to himself, "should you choose to accept it, is to get this bunch of losers to where they wanna be." Even Tom Cruise would have turned this one down, he thought and yet he had done it....that's one in the eye for Scientology he thought!

Back in East Yorkshire, things were about to go badly wrong!

The telephone rang at 6.30 am and a shot of chest-tightening adrenaline pulsed through my still slumbering body. No one ever phones me at 6.30 am not even councillors! 6.30 pm certainly, 11.00 pm regularly, weekends, holidays, during bouts of dysentery occasionally, but never at 6.30 am.

It wasn't that this was a particular sacred part of a Chief Officer's day; it was just that no one I knew got up at 6.30 am. Someone's died, I thought; my head pounding from the sudden awakening. My telephone number having temporarily escaped me, I muttered a sound like "Hello".

"Colin, it's John Papworth."

John was Head of the Policy Unit at the Council, I had mentored him during a top managers' programme, a process which appeared to be most effective when combined with long bouts of drinking in The George Pub.

"Hi, John, what's up?"

"Have you seen the front page of the Guardian?" His question seemed to make as much sense to me as, do you like pineapple or what's the capital of Croatia? Of course I hadn't seen the front page of the Guardian. For God's sake, did they print it this early? They would need to employ sodding vampires. I restrained myself.

"No, John, is it interesting? "

"Are you sitting down?" I thought this was adding insult to injury giving that I would still be lying down but for his phone call.

"Yes, John. What's happened?"

John explained that the newly elected Labour Government was establishing a new good cause for lottery funds, the New Opportunities Fund, and that the Guardian was reporting that the Millennium Commission's funds were being cut to help establish it.

"It lists the projects that won't be getting funding as a result and it mentions The Deep in John Prescott's constituency!"

I thanked John and hung up. John seemed to love passing on bad news, which being a Policy Officer was probably just as well as he had to do it quite a lot. I sat on the edge of my bed. "Bad news?" asked my wife. "Yeah, sort of". I looked at the alarm clock, it was 6.40 am; I felt suddenly very weary. It was going to be a long day.

The morning was spent taking calls from every Guardian reader in the Council, one of which clearly included the Leader. I was summoned immediately to the Guildhall and entered the Chief Executive's Office. Councillor Doyle, normally a calm, spiritual man, looked furious. I threw a glance to the Chief Executive whose body language clearly indicated that he was with the leader on this one!

I couldn't understand the atmosphere, it was by no means certain that the Guardian's report was accurate and, even it was, whilst the project ending would be disappointing, a decision by Government to change the rules at this late stage would clearly not fall into the "Colin's fault" category of problems: indeed some would argue that the Council would come out of this with credit for having tried so hard. Councillor Doyle soon explained!

John Prescott had interpreted the story as an attack on him personally and probably the whole of the new Labour Government. He believed that we had briefed the press and understandably he was furious. He had expressed his feelings to Councillor Doyle that morning and those views were now being passed onto me! Counillor Gemmell would be spoken to personally by the Deputy Prime Minister.

Most of us learn as a child that sometimes it's just best to take the telling off without arguing. This was clearly such an occasion. Pat Doyle looked me in the eye.

"You know this is over now, don't you!" It was not a question.

"Yes, Councillor Doyle" I replied meekly.

"The Deep is dead, it's finished. I want to hear no more about it". He stormed out. More confused than dejected, I made my way back to my office, checked my diary. I had a presentation on The Deep booked for that afternoon at the Chamber of Commerce. I knew that the Hull Daily Mail editor was President and to cancel would only trigger more press speculation; to explain that the Leader had instructed me to stop work on The Deep, would have become a front page story and would have appeared disloyal. It would have been interpreted as me trying to pressurize Pat Doyle into changing his mind. To continue with the talk would, technically at least, go against a direct instruction.

I decided that the most important thing was that 50 or 60 local businessmen had arranged their diaries to attend and that to cancel without notice or reason would be unfair to them.

It was a pleasant enough day at least weather wise, so I strolled the 300 yards down Beverley Road to the Chamber of Commerce's office. I gave my normal presentation, describing the project's story and its aims. Given the audience I explained the business case and our pricing policy, which even back in 1997 was clearly developed. A family of 5 would be able to visit The Deep for less than the cost of a single ticket to the Dome. As ever the presentation was greeted with great enthusiasm – there was something about The Deep that captured the imagination of people, whether they be school children or businessmen people.

I concluded by explaining that, whilst we as yet have no confirmation of that morning's press story, The Deep may not now be able to proceed. I took my seat, sipped at a glass of water and waited for the conventional vote of thanks.

It didn't come in quite the form I expected. The President certainly thanked me but continued by announcing that his paper would now launch a campaign to "Keep The Deep". He asked for the support of the Chamber and it was agreed unanimously.

I had temporarily been removed from the game. It would now be up to others to decide whether The Deep continued. The Council considered it dead, but would the City?

The answer was immediate and dramatic. The Hull Daily Mail's next front page was "Dear Tony, Keep The Deep" and carried an open letter to the Prime Minister. It asked people to write to them and they would pass on the letters to 10 Downing Street. Letters of support arrived from church groups, community groups, businesses and, most touchingly, individuals. All those presentations over the last few years, all those evening trips out to talk to some group or the other had not been in vain. The people had been listening and they at least had cared.

I remember with great affection a short letter from an elderly lady, which simply said, "We've lost so much, don't take away our hope. Keep The Deep."

David meanwhile had gone through his own personal hell. John Prescott had contacted him and expressed his disappointment as only John can. David can hold his own against most people though and he explained that he had had nothing to do with the story and John eventually accepted his word. John Prescott was later to prove one of the best friends The Deep ever had, but for now we were happy for him not to be an enemy.

By the end of that long difficult day the Millennium Commission had circulated a press statement saying that no decisions had yet been made and that those project bids listed remained under consideration.

Of course we never found out where and why the story had started. Or indeed if there had ever been any truth in it. Certainly it seems likely that it emanated from London and that we were unwitting victims, or perhaps beneficiaries, of the perpetrator. Needless to say, I was quietly allowed to continue working on the project.

The episode, short and furious as it was, showed the public support for The Deep in a way which subtly changed the political reality; before The Guardian, The Deep felt like a Council project, afterwards it felt like the City's project.

CHAPTER 12   WINTER 1997/8

THE DECISION

"Nothing succeeds like the appearance of success."

Christopher Lasch

It was November 1997 and we awaited news on whether our bid to the Millennium Commission had been successful. Although we had received some positive noises, there was nothing that could be confidently called a leak and so on that morning the future of the project was in the balance as never before.

At least the decision would be clear-cut. With a successful bid of nearly £18 million the momentum behind the project would be all but unstoppable; without it there would clearly be no way forward.

The arrangement was that we were to be faxed first thing in the morning, directly by the Millennium Commission with the result of our bid. I had arranged for the team to be present in my office so that we could share the moment together. I rose early after a sleepless night and decided to go into work early and check the fax machine was working. It was 7.30 am as I drove along the banks of the Humber; a steel grey sky flashed off the dark waters of the estuary and my mind drifted back to that view of the Humber that David and I had on our first trip to London, - was it really only 2 years ago?

This morning would bring one of only two possible results and each one of them terrified me. If we were successful, there would be no doubt that we would be expected to deliver the project. Despite our outward confidence this still felt like a largely academic exercise. We had filled in the forms, gone through the processes, and argued our case, but the entire life of The Deep could still be contained in a single filing cabinet. On the other hand if we failed, then questions would be asked about the hundreds of thousands of pounds the bid had cost, none of which would now be returned. All we would have to show for our efforts was a pile of wastepaper and 250,000 disappointed residents. I couldn't help but feel that if The Deep were to hit the rails this morning, my career would not be far behind it. I turned on the radio to change the subject of this internal dialogue. It was Radio 4 and on the morning programme, Chris Smith MP, the Minister responsible for Millennium projects, was being interviewed.

"Good morning and here in the studio with us we have Chris Smith, the Minister responsible for Culture, Media and Sport who today will be announcing the successful bids for this the final round of Millennium Commission projects. Mr Smith, good morning."

"Good morning".

"Now later on this morning you are going to announce the last round of major capital projects for the Millennium Commission, can you tell us what you hope these projects will achieve?"

"Yes, thank you, this is a very exciting day for a number of cities and towns around the country who have put in some tremendous work over the previous months in preparing what are some very imaginative projects which I think will help regenerate some of the most needy parts of the country. We have successful projects in Rotherham". Oh my God, I thought, he`s going to announce them here and he`s already mentioned Magna.

Please Chris say Hull!

"We have a magnificent project in Cornwall which will be telling the story of plant life throughout the world"

Oh my God, he`s mentioned The Eden Project....please Chris say Hull, say The Deep.

"We have projects celebrating Science in Leicester and the arts in Salford."

That's The National Space Centre and the Lowry..... PLEASE GOD, MAKE HIM SAY HULL!

"As well as many other imaginative projects throughout the country."

He didn't say Hull.

Surely if we had been successful Hull would have been on Chris Smith's list. If just because of the connection with John Prescott or the fact that Hull is normally seen by the rest of the country as a deserving case, it would have been the perfect political example to use, there could only be one explanation, we had failed.

By the time I reached the office I had convinced myself that there may be another explanation. Perhaps we were one of the many other imaginative schemes he had referred to. If we ever needed a stroke of luck - and we had needed many in the project to date , we needed one now.

I was the first in the office that morning and checked the fax machine. It snoozed quietly to itself; I pulled up a chair and sat staring at it, willing it to awaken. A few minutes later it hiccupped, burped and began to eat a new piece of A4 for its breakfast.

As the text came out I tried to read the first few words upside down, it was junk mail. Clearly someone in an insurance company's marketing department had thought that the best way to impress potential customers was to send them a blurred page of type, to get the customer to pay for the paper and to do it at a time that would give the recipient an adrenaline rush of bungee-jumping proportions. A further 15 minutes of watching and waiting followed until the machine once more whirred in to life. It was the Millennium Commission's logo that I saw first followed by the words, "We are pleased to inform you…!"

The fax continued: £17.83 million. I took the piece of paper, read it through and went through into my office and sat down. I was the only person in Hull to know that The Deep would now be built. If there was ever a moment in the project at which the dream became a reality, it was now. For those few moments alone I was filled with a mixture of excitement and fear, we had a chance to address all the major agendas of this proud city, regeneration, image, education and to provide it with a symbol of its future. All we had to do now was raise the other £20 million, appoint all the consultants, design a world-class attraction and then open it and run it at a profit for ever.

Not unexpectedly, David Gemmell was the first to join me in the office. Like me, he hadn't been able to sleep and decided to pre-empt the meeting by a good half hour. He came in looking breathless and white. "Any news?" He asked. I slid the paper along the desk and he read it quickly. "We've bloody done it." he cried. We both stood up and hugged. It was the only time in my life I've ever felt the need to cuddle a councillor (particularly one as bearded as this one).

Not wanting to tempt fate again, but mainly due to an innately cheap personality I had a single bottle of champagne ready. When Nick, Gill and Carl arrived, we toasted each other and raised our plastic cups to The Deep. These youngsters, as well as many others including (in truth) it must be said a number of Councillors, had shown an imagination and commitment to their jobs which it is still unfashionable to expect from the public sector, particularly local government. There would be no bonuses for those involved, no special awards, there would be many who would go unsung to this day, but they have the satisfaction of knowing they had made it happen.

A few days earlier I had prepared two press releases, one which included a quote from me which expressed how disappointed we were to have come so far and failed, and another with a quote from the Leader of the Council, which said how pleased he was that Hull had been successful. I now happily released the more positive of the two press releases.

The phone began to ring soon after 9 am as news spread first amongst colleagues and then wider afield. Some of the congratulations which we received from time-served officers who had had little or nothing to do with the bid were the most touching. One sensed that something in The Deep or in what it represented had touched people at all levels in the organisation; they had after all, it seemed, been willing us on, quietly wishing us well.

David and I had to rush away to Leeds for a Millennium Commission publicity gathering and so we quickly arranged to meet the rest of the team later that evening and to celebrate properly.

In Leeds we were embarrassed to find that other projects had stands with complex models, logos and visuals of their projects as well as large teams of staff in attendance. We had almost nothing. We realised that these projects must have expected to be successful, whereas we hadn't really dared to hope. As for the badges, balloons and T shirts they were giving away we had nothing. We had been on such a restricted budget that we had no money for such luxuries, spending every penny we had on our bid. We left feeling a bit deflated, like boys trying to play a man's game. David picked up on my mood. "Don't worry, son, our time will come!"

He was right of course, for although at the time we had felt amateurish, almost naked without our own little coloured logo to show off, we had always felt that if a logo is to truly represent what The Deep stands for, our brand if you like, it needs to be informed by the product, and we didn't yet have a product fully enough developed to do that.

We also felt rather than knew that there would be more to the development of a brand than the design of a logo. Until we understood what that was, we would just have to live with not having car stickers and lapel badges to give away.

By now the afternoon was drawing on and we were both eager to get back. Apart from wanting to know how news of the successful bid was playing in the city, tonight was the switch on of Hull's Christmas lights and David as Chairman of Tourism would be expected to be there and then to join other Councillors at the annual Chamber of Commerce buffet, whilst I had agreed to meet the bid team for a celebratory drink and meal.

As twilight dimmed to a dark November evening it was clear that neither Dave nor I would make our rendezvous. Having discovered too late that the only restaurants still available to us involved us in driving through them, we instead agreed that I would pick up the bid team and David would try to sneak us, uninvited, into the buffet reception. We would arrive after the speeches and if we kept a low profile, a few more guests, a few less sausage rolls wouldn't matter.

Two hours later I led a small sheepish project group into the hotel lounge. For the briefest of moments the room went quiet, I looked for someone to speak to, to ask permission, to explain our gate-crashing but before I could do so the Chairman, Councillors, and all the great and the good of the City present stood as one and applauded us.

CHAPTER 13
SPRING 1998

AFTER THE NEWS

"I am returning this otherwise good writing paper to you because someone has printed gibberish all over it and put your name at the top."
  An Ohio University Professor

The following morning I felt like a new father with a week-old baby. By now the news was widely known; all the congratulatory calls had come in and I found myself flipping through my old address books to find ex-colleagues who I could bore with the news.

Again, like a new father, I had no idea what to do with this new creature and had little desire to move from celebratory mode to the sleepless night phase.

The project entered a strange torpor; we had close on £18 million, a site and an outline design; however there were still a few small details to settle like the fact that we remained about £20 million short, that we lacked any sort of management Board or infrastructure to take the project on from here, and we now had less than 3 years to build The Deep before the Millennium Commissions deadline of 31st December 2001.

Before we could address these issues the University began to take a much more vigorous interest. Until now almost all communications had been through Professor Jack Hardisty whose Humber Observatory was to provide scientific credibility to The Deep. Suddenly it seemed, the University realised that it was now something of an unwitting partner in a highly speculative visitor attraction, having had little or no internal debate as to its role, obligations, exposure or its research strategy.

All communications, we were told, would now be via Trevor Newsom, a walrus of a man who it appeared, had been briefed to re-examine the project from top to bottom, perhaps with a view to withdrawal. In a later telephone conversation with David Gemmell, Trevor implied as much.

We had no choice now but to spend valuable time and energy dealing with Trevor's questions, most of which had of course already been discussed in detail with the

Millennium Commission and been debated and resolved in a hundred partners meetings previously. Hour after hour we spent justifying every aspect of the project to the University. If we thought that receiving the Millennium Commission grant would galvanise our partners we were wrong. Only now that it began to look as if we might actually succeed did they really engage, but now it felt as if the agenda was to find a way out, whilst avoiding getting the blame for The Deep's demise. Luckily, as busy as I was, Trevor's own workload at the University was greater still and given his style of work it was clear that something would soon have to give. We, on the other hand, were beginning to become frustrated at the University playing Devil's advocate without making any contribution to the workload. They were after all a partner, and that had to mean more than constantly questioning the work of others.

Whilst Trevor had a particular talent for producing frustration in others, he did unknowingly serve one vital role. He introduced us to Dr Giles Davidson!

Following the Millennium grant news, the Council's Chief Executive, had rightly decided that the time was now right to appoint a shadow Board which would establish a new charitable organisation to take the project forward and to begin the process of making The Deep an independent body, separate from the Council. Such an embryonic Board would need a company secretary. So Trevor proposed seconding his assistant, Giles Davidson, to the role. This way Trevor, and the University, would have a set of eyes and ears at the heart of the project.

A few days later Giles arrived at Ferensway and I ran through the bones of the project and our current position. Giles was an administrator at the University but a marine biologist by training; a young man in his early 30's, he was a direct descendant of Trotsky and a relation of the erotic underwear magnet Janet Reger, a strange combination of genes in anyone's book!

Physically he was a big man, tall, well built with incongruously spiked black hair. Although he had something of the pedant about him, in other respects he could not have been more different to Trevor. We established him in a small grubby office and he began to work... and work... and work.

Within a few weeks it was clear that Giles was regularly working 12, even 16-hour days; his car arrived so early and left so late that others thought it had been abandoned. He was popular, good company, articulate and extremely intelligent.

Giles, like so many others in this story, was the right person at the right time. His arrival gave me vital support at a key time. From now on, Giles and I would work as a team.

One of our first tasks was to establish the embryonic Board.

Until now we had stumbled through our decision-making processes using a number of ad-hoc arrangements. We had briefly used a working party of the key council chairmen, Councillors Bradley (Chair of Planning), Stanley (Technical Services) and of course Gemmell.

More successfully we had called what we pretentiously called summit meetings, involving the University's Vice Chancellor, David Dilks, and Professor Chesters together with the Council's own Leader, Chief Executive and Chief Legal Officer. It was now time, however, for the child to begin to become independent. It was time to create a completely new organisation.

Giles undertook the establishment of the charity, which for no apparent reason was named The European Maritime Institute in Hull. Within weeks we were advised that we could not call ourselves an institute or European without fulfilling a raft of other conditions so we became simply EMIH.

The Shadow Board was to consist of 6 members, 3 from the University and 3 from the Council with the Council holding the Chair. Due to the legislation concerning local authority controlled companies only one of the Council's places could be taken by a Councillor or officer, leaving 2 spaces for outside nominees.

David suggested we ask Jack Brignall, a local property developer. He was one of the City's most successful businessmen, a past Chairman of the Hanson Trust and now owner of Wykeland Developments. Jack was committed to Hull and was one of few entrepreneurs who was both trusted and respected by the Councillors.

Jack was in his early 70s, fit-looking, and his pleasant manner and frugal office gave no clue as to his successful business career. Jack agreed to join the Board as a Trustee; he was particularly interested in our plans for a Business Centre. His office on the third floor of Wykeland House was on the opposite bank of the River Hull to The Deep and commanded the best view in the City of our chosen site. Jack agreed to let us use his office for meetings which allowed the board to remain focused and monitor progress.

Jack was listed by The Sunday Times as being one of the richest men in the Country. He always denied it of course, so I have no way of knowing if that was the case. What I am sure of is that he was one of the wisest and most modest men I have had the pleasure of working with and we all came to rely on his opinion.

With Councillor Gemmell the obvious choice for the Councillor representative and Chair, we asked Mike Killoran to join the Board as the Council's third nominee. Mike's £1,000 contribution had kicked the project off in the early days and he would bring a commercial edge and energy to the Shadow Board.

The University nominated Professor Graham Chesters, another key player in the genesis of the project, as well as Professor Ekkehard Kopp, a professor of Maths and finally John Parkes CBE, the previous Chief Executive of Humberside County Council and an accountant by profession. John was insightful, intelligent and had that old fashioned attribute, honour, in bucket loads. The Chairman asked John to be his Deputy, and he agreed.

Each side also nominated an observer to the Board, it was me for the Council and Trevor Newsom for the University. Giles was company secretary and now carried the greatest burden for pushing the project forward. With Neil Porteus our adopted financial whiz kid who had become more and more involved with the project over recent months, as Finance Director, The Deep began its journey to independence.

With the Shadow Board now in place, the earlier excitement of the good news began to wear off as Giles and I realised we were left with no project team to take The Deep forward. Architects, Exhibition designers, quantity surveyors, engineers etc all had been given contracts which terminated the moment the bid was submitted. The Council's technical staff changed the habit of a lifetime and moved quickly to appoint BDP as project managers who were then told to begin a whole new appointment process starting with an architect.

The opportunity to revisit the design was not lost on a number of stakeholders and they soon began to bring their own agendas for The Deep to the table, notably City Vision whose support and funds had always been vital. They expressed their strongly held view that The Deep needed a signature architect.

Whilst it was great to see the City's ambition for the project begin to grow, it was also somewhat frustrating. We had delivered what was considered by many to have been impossible and we had done so at comparatively little cost to the City. Now though it seemed that not only did the City want it for free, they wanted it better. It was like Crewe Alexandra winning the Premiership only for their supporters to demand the Champions League! Giles summed it up when he said," I feel like we've climbed Everest without oxygen and just as we reach the summit we get a message from base camp complaining that we should have taken a bigger flag."

I have to admit to also being less than enthusiastic about seeking to appoint new architects. A new architect would mean writing off all the design work done to date; it would obviously mean a new building design and no doubt a new exhibition storyline and it followed that in turn it would probably result in a delay of at least six months.

The costings we had were for the building we had, so we would also have to hope that our new Architect could follow a budget.

The Millennium Commission had told us that the project had to be completed (but not necessarily opened) by the end of the Millennium Year 2001 or they may choose to exercise their right to reclaim their grant, and the same seemed true of any ERDF funding we received. An initial programme showed that even if we started immediately we would be lucky to finish by mid-2001. A delay whilst we redesigned the building might put back completion until the end of 2001 at the earliest and so any further unforeseen delays and the consequences could prove to be catastrophic.

Such a dramatic change of horse mid-stream would, however, not only affect the programme and budget but may have jeopardised the whole delicate partnership on which the project was built. Without Deep Sea World's Architects, Buttress, Fuller, Alsop and Williams, I doubted if I could keep an increasingly distracted Phil Crane on the project. Even our relationship with the National History Museum could be at risk, as new architects would also mean that we would lose our exhibition designers - and their involvement in the project seemed to matter greatly to the NHM.

This was a disconcerting change; our promise to deliver a Millennium project at little or no cost to the Council had been predicated on the understanding that others would not increase the ambition for the project at a key moment. I couldn't help but feel that the closer the project moved towards David's vision the further it moved away from my ability to deliver it. Quite suddenly, the City's ambition for The Deep had increased. From now on quality would be an even more important aspect to our work than ever before. A quality building, with quality displays, quality education, catering, finishes, marketing, everything was expected to be the best, unfortunately no one thought to tell the budget.

CHAPTER 14   SUMMER 1998

PORTUGAL

"The only good ideas are the ones I can take the credit for."

R.Stevens

I know some people who think that where a Council is twinned with is an important factor in applying for jobs. Hence being twinned with Georgetown, Jamaica is a definite plus in the overall recruitment package; even if you never go, the potential of a "Cultural Exchange" hangs in the air with all the promise of frying bacon.

This however is seldom a huge incentive for interviewees in Hull, twinned as it is with Rotterdam where the container ships come from, Reykjavik in Iceland where the Arctic wind comes from and Freetown, Sierra Leone where all the colourful diseases come from.

Indeed, for several years it was so rare for a deputation to Freetown to return without at least one serious medical condition that an invitation to go was about as welcome as the black spot and triggered rumours that Personnel were using it as a cheap way to trim the workforce.

When it was proposed then, that we should attend Lisbon's Expo '98 it was only with a mixture of excitement and wariness that I accepted.

My only other experience of a Council-sponsored jolly had been a few years before. That had been in the winter of 1994 when Poland was first emerging from communism. I had been invited for a cultural exchange visit to Szczecin on the Polish/German border (never a particularly safe place to be) along with my then Chairman, a hyperactive choreographer and his brooding wife plus a few others.

The trip had not begun well from the moment we arrived at the so called 'hotel', which turned out to be a former KGB safe house. The visit had however taken a rather unfortunate turn for the worse when our touchingly polite guide explained how much of Szczecin had only recently been redeveloped after the war. I had enquired with due solemnity whether the Luftwaffe had done much damage and was told with no hint of anger, "No, none, it was the R.A.F."

At the formal dinner that first evening we were served what I later learnt was Steak Tartar, a raw egg on a bed of raw fatty mincemeat. Not surprisingly for a choreographer who thought that even sitting in the same room as a recipe book would add an inch to his waist line, my Chairman pushed the offering away with undisguised revulsion, quickly followed by the rest of our group. In an effort to avoid a diplomatic incident I decided to make the effort. Later that night in my Polish non-en-suite bedroom I realised the magnitude of my error. I spent the next 12 hours being so sick I was afraid I would die; this was followed by another 12 hours of being so sick I was afraid I wouldn't! Never was a Hull City Tourist Information Centre carrier bag put to better use.

But Portugal was not Poland and there was, therefore, an end-of-term feel about our drive to Manchester Airport. We were on our way to Lisbon but not to some worthy conference or stressful sales drive, but to visit the biggest party in Europe, Expo '98. Its theme was the sea, and with David, Giles D and Keith German (our recently appointed Project Manager), the company would be as pleasant as the weather would undoubtedly be. Life was good!

We had seen our hotel room in a brochure; it was modern and well equipped. We would eat no bits of uncooked animal. Portugal was going to be great!

It was in fact hot! The airport was hot, the customs hall was hot, and even the air-conditioned Mercedes, which drove us to our hotel, was hot. The receptionist on the other hand was real cool. She turned from her computer screen and flashed a mischievous smile. "No, I'm afraid I have no reservation for a Mr Gemmell, I have a Mr Brown, Mr Davison, Mr Ger-main and a Mr Jem-el" "That's me, that's me!" said David. "Jem-el, Superman's uncle". "Good, here are your keys, rooms 102, 3, 4 and 5. Have a nice stay gentleman".

Like kids who couldn't wait to get to the beach, twenty minutes later we had changed, freshened up and were assembled back in the hotel lobby.

The Lisbon Metro was newly built, it was clean, efficient and deserted, a 10-minute ride and we arrived at Expo '98. The station was stunning, soaring spaces framed with glass and white steel covered inter-locking levels of concourse. We grabbed a baguette and began to explore, making notes as we went; it was like a theme park idea shop.

Lisbon '98 was built on a massive urban regeneration site on the banks of the River Tagus. In both scale and ambition it was enormous, it was a whole town of exhibits, cafes, shows and shops all based around the theme of the Oceans.

We began at the Sea Pavilion. Themed as an underwater laboratory, it used models, audio visual displays and text to tell the story of the Deep Sea. A long circular route wound around a large central feature; around the outer walls projections told the story of evolution, black smokers and the abyssal plain. It could not have been a better example of what we had in mind for The Deep. All around us a tide of visitors trotted down the ramp.

I turned from the exhibits. "Err team, I hate to say this but no one is paying any attention." Sure enough, this was the closest we had yet been to seeing our vision of The Deep and to the visitors it was merely a route way. We waited until the stream of people had passed; searching their faces initially for enthusiasm, then for interest and eventually, it seemed, for consciousness. Eventually we followed too, as we reached the end of the descent we turned towards the exit and met a crowd pushing to get close to what from a distance looked like a large upturned glass bowl; inside, jelly fish pulsed on a current of circulating water. The first live exhibit of our visit and it had grabbed the visitors like nothing else.

Outside again it was not only the heat which hit as but the intense eye-watering light of the early afternoon sun. It reflected off the polished building surfaces, it was mirrored from the River Tagus; it penetrated our heads and triggered the second largest area in a man's brain. "Fancy a beer?" said Keith. In the shade of a canopied patio area we sat and drank what tasted like the best cold beer I've ever had from a plastic glass. Keith, ever the professional, opened our guide book to the map and spread it open on the white plastic table.

"We've only got this afternoon and tomorrow morning, and in that time we have got to see the Aquarium and the Virtual Reality Pavilion, anything else will be a bonus." Keith continued, "What if we finish these and go straight to the VR Pavilion, then that will leave us enough time to get a bite to eat and we can do the Aquarium tomorrow."

We all agreed: time was of the essence. There was not a moment to spare. "Anyone for another beer?" asked Giles. "Yeah, go on then!" we all chorused.

It was gone three by the time we found our way to the start of the very long queue to see the VR Pavilion. As the afternoon wore on we shuffled yard by painful yard forward, behind us the queue grew longer still. Giles checked the guide book. "It says here that the VR Pavilion closes at 5.00 pm. They wouldn't let us stand in line if we weren't going to get in, would they? With luck we should only have a maximum of what, another 20 minutes to wait." He closed the guide book with a flourish and smiled, case proved!

Back in Hull however, the Lucky Little Devil was enjoying his holiday from us as well. He sipped his Baileys and switched his hotel room TV to one of the adult channels. "Life was indeed good" he thought. "But I'm still probably better off without it! I wonder how the boys are doing without me!"

Three and a quarter hours later the queue shuffled forward one last time and we entered the VR Pavilion which had, it transpired been staying open until 10.00 pm every night to cope with the crowds.

The Pavilion used computer animations in various forms to take visitors on a fantasy journey into strange and futuristic oceans. The show was pulsed with groups of about 20 visitors being passed on from one 'guide' to the next, each with their own carefully rehearsed script, each taking us deeper into the fantasy, The illusion was suddenly shattered however when one young female guide suddenly deviated from her well-worn script which exhorted us to "Stay away from the water-tight doors as the external pressure this far down could buckle the atomic sub's superstructure if tampered with" and suddenly began an incongruous conversation with an elderly English couple about how much she had enjoyed her year studying English in Guildford.

I saw Giles glance over at me and roll his eyes; the lesson was clear, heavily themed attractions always proved vulnerable to human beings. Maintaining an illusion about actually being under the sea was probably not possible, not only because of ill-trained staff but simply, people aren't stupid, they know that any such illusion is fake and no amount of artificial rock or luminous yellow danger signs could reasonably be expected to convince anyone differently.

Fantasy may attract enough interest to have people queuing for five hours, but achieving it with any degree of integrity was going to be nigh on impossible.

That evening we sat together in the last of the Expo eateries still open and in the welcome cool of the Lisbon evening. In the distance fireworks signalled that night's closure of Expo. We ate another open sandwich, had a final beer and discussed the day's lessons.

We had learnt the importance of being able to display real animals. We had learnt that, whilst fantasy was popular, it was also very difficult to pull off, and we had learnt the importance of the guide /public interaction.

We had also learnt that the queues in this place could be long, slow and hot and so we determined that tomorrow we would ensure that we would arrive as soon as the park opened and go straight to the Aquarium. With any luck we would be able to go straight in.

Next morning we arrived as per our schedule and strolled through the various exhibition pavilions towards the aquarium. As we did so, we began to sense that everyone else was heading in the same direction. Our pace picked up to a brisk walk before becoming an undignified rush. We joined the queue and quickly saw it snake away behind us. An almost imperceptible wave of expectation spread through the line. The aquarium had opened its doors. We had in fact arrived well before opening time and yet we still had to queue for 4 hours. It was so busy that they had had to divide the route through the aquarium into two separate journeys so even after a 4-hour wait we would only be allowed to see half of the exhibition.

The aquarium was, nonetheless, beautiful but was still essentially a living art gallery; it had little interpretation and no interactivity. It did, however, have a stunning central tank, its depth, breadth and realistic rockscaping created an awesome backdrop for its species. Cow nose rays glided in formation in an aquatic ballet as large sharks patrolled their domain. In some of the smaller tanks bejewelled Leafy Sea Dragons swayed to a silent waltz. Sea Otters rolled on their back and cracked open a crab. I accused David of calling them Sea Badgers, he hadn't, but Sea Badgers became the accepted shorthand between us both for our combined lack of any zoological background.

Apart from the animals it was the water quality and colour which struck us most. It was the clearest most perfect blue. Shafts of clear sapphire light penetrating the tank.

We didn't know how but we knew then that we wanted that for The Deep.

Whilst it was difficult to draw too many conclusions from such a facility, we were deeply impressed by the need to have a single major tank and to view it from as many aspects as possible rather than to opt for many less dramatic tanks. We learnt that quality counts in terms of rockscaping and water treatment and above all we were reassured that people like aquariums….a lot! But we also realised that The Deep could never compete with Lisbon, at least not if it attempted to do so on Lisbon's terms. If, as some were beginning to argue, The Deep was to be just an aquarium it would indeed be just that, just another aquarium. Our budget would not buy us a Lisbon and playing catch up was not really what Hull had in mind for its new icon. We would need to build a new type of aquarium. Lisbon reminded us that we had to stick with our original vision. Lisbon showed us that it could work.

CHAPTER 15   AUTUMN 1998

OUT WITH THE OLD

"A Doctor can bury his mistakes but an Architect can only advise his client to plant vines."

Frank Lloyd Wright.

As soon as news of our progress spread into the outside world, so everyone with even a vaguely related product began to get in touch, carpet for the offices, cutlery for the Café, even fossil replicas for the shop. All of which were about 3 years too early. Most of these I passed on to our new Project Manager, Keith German. Most but not all, because, given how dependent we were on keeping local support, I always tried to at least be polite when local chancers, or in some cases loonies insisted on talking to me about how they should be involved in some way.

"There's a local Business man wants to talk to you. Says his name is Jeremy Lee", bellowed Lorraine.

Unknown Businessmen was one category of people I really didn't enjoy talking to. I thought I knew most of the Business leaders in the City and if, as in this case, I didn't recognise the name, this normally meant that for Businessman you could read a salesman trying to sell me something I didn't want ,didn't need and probably couldn't afford, but which I had every likelihood of buying anyway. I am after all the only man I know to haggle in an Egyptian market only to end up paying more than the original asking price. I reluctantly took the call.

"Good Morning can I help?"

"Mr Brown, my name is Jeremy Lee, I run a business over on the South Bank and we make Aquariums, I wonder if we could meet?"

I carried on signing some timesheets as I tried to politely explain that we were not in the market for hobbyist aquarium tanks and that this was a serious, large-scale project. The caller however was not responding to polite and so I quickly reverted to type.

"With all respect, Mr Lee, it is unlikely that a company from where did you say, Barton upon Humber, could be of any help." Jeremy still persisted. I was tempted for a moment to buy a little aquarium from him for my living room, just to shut him up, but I rallied.

I decided to try and impress him with my new-found knowledge of the international aquarium industry.

"I'm sorry, Mr Lee, but this is difficult to explain without being rude, but you may have heard of a new aquarium just opened in Lisbon, it's been in the news lately, it has tanks containing over three million litres, and housing a hundred different species. That's the sort of Aquarium we're talking about!"

"Yes, that's right; my company did all the water treatment systems for it. And - not that it's important but it's Doctor Lee."

I put down my pen, and paused for a second or two. Sheepishly I asked, "Where did you say you were again?"

As soon as we could arrange to meet I travelled across the Humber Bridge and Jeremy showed me around his offices. His company was called I.A.T. standing for International Aquarium Technology and they had designed and installed the water treatment systems for some of the best aquariums in the world. In doing so, they had also learned a fair bit about the exhibition design and animal husbandry issues.

Up until now we had no idea where, how or indeed if we could get hold of any actual fish for our Aquarium and, if we could get hold of them, then how would we keep them alive. With a new architect now on the horizon it would mean that Phil Crane's architect would no longer be required and that meant that there was every likelihood that Deep Sea World would also pull out leaving us with no links in the industry and no knowledge about fish. Although not an expert (see Sea Badgers above) I had suspected for some time that fish could be a key ingredient in a successful aquarium and that knowing how to get them and keep them would be useful skills to have in the project team.

Jeremy might just be able to provide a way to access these skills.

The Lucky Little Devil had arrived back from his extended vacation and had (although he said so himself) pulled off quite a coup. In a sleepy little village outside of Barton and less than 20 minutes drive from Hull, in a place that felt like it would consider The Wicker Man to be a documentary, in this most unlikely yet convenient of locations we had stumbled across one of the world's leading aquarium specialists.

Even at our first meeting Jeremy had been surprised to learn that, as yet, we did not have a managing operator and that we only had the most informal of arrangements with Phil Crane and so we resolved that we should begin to formalise the role of the managing operator as quickly as possible. There were still too many unknowns to let a contract to manage the facility once it had been opened, and so it was decided that in the interim we would let a formal contract for operational advice in the design process. By continuing to have a private operator of visitor attractions, particularly aquariums, working with us, we hoped to avoid the more obvious 'white elephant traps' that so many such projects seemed to have blundered into.

The interviews took place in Jack Brignall's office. Running aquariums is a pretty specialised business and the field was small, so Jack, Trevor Newsom and I set aside a single day for the interviews. First in was Ian Cunningham, one of the original founders of the Sea Life chain, which was subsequently sold on and is now part of the Merlin mega chain. Ian and his partner David Mace currently owned a company called Real Life Leisure, which ran the aquarium of the Lakes in Cumbria and the Oceanarium in Bournemouth. After some encouragement from us they had decided to bid as a joint venture with Dr Jeremy Lee.

Ian had, he said, become bored with the production line approach of Sea Life centres and now wanted to build a small family of unique aquarium-based attractions. The Deep would be a major corner stone in that chain.

Phil Crane followed Ian into the interview and his long-held suspicions about the University were strengthened by Trevor Newsom's aggressive, almost confrontational style. Before long, he had had enough and withdrew from the process. I walked with him to the door, and outside into the street, across the way was Sammy's Point, the site for The Deep that we had visited together almost exactly two years previously.

He was bowing out, he said, he now had to concentrate on his new project, Blue Planet, and he would not work in a subordinate relationship with University staff that had never had to run anything to make money in their lives. I considered explaining the challenges of financing a modern university but decided against it.

We shook hands and said goodbye; Phil wished me luck. He had been with the project almost from the beginning; to a large extent it had been his idea to incorporate an aquarium. I'd miss him, but God he'd been hard work at times. A few weeks later we returned his £16,000 contribution which had been so important to us just 18 months earlier.

Politically we now needed to replace Phil with another private partner who would show enough commercial belief in the operational phase to ensure that the Council and the University would still have the confidence to make that final commitment and move from design work to construction. Ian and Real Life Leisure were ideal, and so, to cement our new partnership, David Gemmell and I arranged to take him to dinner the following week after he had had an opportunity to brief his partner. The meal, ironically at a Sea Food Restaurant proved that this new relationship would be no easier than the one with Phil which it was meant to replace.

Over the last few months, a number of earlier and perhaps more problematic projects had become operational. The Earth Centre at Doncaster, designed, judging from its rank of entry control gates, to rival Disneyland Paris in popularity had had less customers than a Hog Roast at a Synagogue's fun day. Whilst frustratingly for the Millennium Commission, similar projects which had had nothing to do with them such as the Leeds Armouries were also attracting criticism. Millennium grants were beginning to be seen in some quarters as millstones rather than mile stones! Personally I wasn't worried that all Millennium Projects would be lumped together as failures. After all it was still only 1998 and I was sure that when the New Millennium Dome was opened, the press would stop their criticism! Nevertheless, it did seem that these recent failures had begun to influence Ian Cunningham's views, or perhaps it was simply that he wanted to keep the upper hand in the design discussions which he knew would soon follow. My own guess is that Ian's initial enthusiasm for the project had not been matched by his partner and a bit of re-positioning was going on. Whatever the reason, by the end of the meal it was clear that we appeared to have swapped one reluctant partner for another. We would have to show Ian - and probably more likely his business partner- that we were serious about building something which could be commercially successful. If he saw that, perhaps his attitude may improve.

A few days later a few key Board members, Keith, Giles and I gathered at the University to choose an architect. The interviews were conducted openly and fairly. Buttress Fuller Alsop & Williams dissipated much of the goodwill felt towards them by appearing still to be in mourning for their original design. Others arrived with models in the shape of everything from Rays to Starfish, with clearly no thought of form following function.

Finally, Sir Terry Farrell and his team presented. Terry was nothing like what I had expected. True, he wore the slightly discordant clothes of a designer confident in his reputation and ability, but his presentation was at once informal and professional. His team were clearly well briefed and prepared but Terry himself seemed almost chatty, as if he were only then beginning to play with the possibilities. He spoke of the relationship between the site and the City and of what makes an icon. Finally, he gave some examples of other buildings he had designed, spoke of his enthusiasm for the project and offered to discuss his fee, if that was a problem (it was!).

It was not the most contentious meeting David had ever had to Chair; the decision was unanimous; above all it was the quality of thought which had impressed. Terry had come across as democratic, open to the views of others and as a bonus he was definitely a signature architect. The panel also felt that he would be a challenge to work with. For us as a client team, we would have to be up to this, and be prepared for some constructive conflict, which we felt could only benefit the project.

As for the exhibition designers, Words and Ideas, who had originally been recommended by Dr Giles Clark at the Natural History Museum, they were another casualty in the round of tenders and interviews which followed. They were replaced by MET Studios, exhibition designers who were commissioned to produce a whole new concept design.

In a replay of the Deep-Sea Leisure/Buttress Fuller situation, the Natural History Museum, or more correctly, its marketing department, then decided that it did not want to risk its reputation and logo on a visitor attraction, particularly now that we had dispensed with their recommended designers, Words and Ideas. Despite our efforts to keep Dr Giles Clarke in particular with us, the Natural History Museum then withdrew as well. I couldn't help wondering if all the fine words from the Natural History Museum that one of its aims was to encourage a wider understanding of science, and to recognise its national obligation to those taxpayers who might not normally have access to their institution, were only worth acting upon if they also happened to be in the interests of its marketing department.

As the Natural History Museum waved goodbye to The Deep, we also said a reluctant farewell to Dr Giles Clarke. Again, a key individual at the beginning of the project left, just when all the hard work looked like paying off.

In effect the original partnership had collapsed, leaving just the Council and a still reticent University, but surprisingly no one seemed to care. The Deep now had a life of its own, not to mention £17 million, and whereas the loss of two such key partners would have been fatal not long ago, now the news was taken in our stride, and it was time to move on.

There was indeed little time for regret. We needed to complete our new team and get it working together quickly. Whilst we now had a significant amount of grant aid in place, we still lacked some £18m and with the binning of the original design and of the undersea research station concept, we were pretty much starting the design phase from scratch.

Keith German, the Project Manager, suggested that we call a two-day design workshop to introduce the new team to each other and to begin to develop a new story. It did not begin well. Real Life Leisure objected to Alex from Met Studio coming and argued that, if we were serious about taking their advice on displays, no exhibition designer was necessary at all.

Giles Davidson had, partly to send a message to our newly appointed team that we intended to squeeze the best value we could from our funds, booked the empty halls of residence at the University for accommodation. The rooms were frugal, clean, warm, and, I thought, adequate for our needs, a view which it immediately became apparent was not shared by our friends from Real Life Leisure.

The meeting room was set out with a series of tables arranged in an oblong with myself, Giles and Keith along one side and Ian, David Mace and Jeremy Lee on the other. It soon took on the atmosphere of cease-fire negotiations rather than team-building. David began by formally complaining about the accommodation and informed us that he was ready to walk off of the project if this was an indication of the way we would run things. It was soon clear that we could expect no brainstorming today; instead we were in for fog and drizzle.

Eventually everyone agreed to blame Giles (except Giles of course) and following suitable soothing noises, the meeting stumbled on. Alex from Met Studios continued to ring every 15 minutes to see if the contract he had won was going to be honoured, and in between placating him we also eventually convinced Ian and David that, having technically appointed Alex before them, we should at least give him a chance to see what he could do.

We tried to explain that we were not building another Sea Life Centre and that our vision and ambition for the project was far greater than this. It was a vision of wet and dry exhibits interacting, using each where appropriate, telling the story of the world's oceans, and that it would be educationally and scientifically robust. Our partners' and funders' ambition for the project extended further than for it to be just another fish zoo.

Whilst this was not new to anyone in the room, there was clearly a fundamental disagreement even at this strategic level, with Ian supporting David, but in more conciliatory tones, and Jeremy Lee clearly much more enthusiastic about the whole concept, and wanting to move forward.

David Mace then brought the meeting to a sudden halt. "Would you mind us having a short break, whilst my colleagues and I consult privately?" Keith and I exchanged glances. "No please take as long as you need." I held out an arm indicating the door. David, Ian and Jeremy left. With our "operating partners" outside the room, there was a general rush to release the frustrations of the morning.

"What the hell are they up to, do they want to be part of this or not?" was the general tone. The question was whether, when they returned, it would merely be to announce their withdrawal from the "team". A few minutes later the door swung open and the three conspirators returned. David was the first to speak. "We've decided to suspend our joint venture relationship and to allow each party to concentrate on what it does best. Real Life will continue to provide operational advice to the project, allowing IAT to deal with the technical design issues."

Our response should have been that a contract had been bid for and won as a joint venture and that, if this was now being dissolved, then we would go out to tender again. Both Real Life Leisure who clearly still had reservations, and IAT who did not, could then have bid separately. However, putting this new team together had put us way behind schedule, we needed to move on. The main loser of this arrangement was IAT; after all, they had won at least part of a contract and now were giving that up in the hope of winning a contract which had yet to be let: did Jeremy realise this?, I wondered

The rest of the day became a process to survive rather than a productive use of time. After an evening spent incongruously in the Students' Union bar, the next day was spent introducing the project and its history to the rest of our new consultant team. Architect, Structural Engineers, Quantity Surveyors, Electrical and Mechanical Engineers and others, each expert in their own field, each clearly fired with enthusiasm for a project which offered more than the run of the mill.

Interestingly, as the meeting wound up, Real Life Leisure representatives became both more positive and less arrogant. We began to suspect that together such an array of experts was more than they were used to dealing with and that our protestations as to our ambition had in some way not really been believed until now.

Whilst the atmosphere had improved we had had little time to make any progress on what for me was the vital issue of developing the storyline; we arranged a smaller meeting to discuss this in Hull the following week. It is strange that given how difficult it was to develop our story that we never seriously considered not having one. The majority of similar attractions may have a theme but few have a story and yet this was always vital to our concept from that initial conversation on the train all those months ago.

We met at the Guildhall, Ian Cunningham, Alex, Julian Tolliss from Terry Farrell's, Giles, Keith and I. Alex had brought Miranda McQuitty with him. Miranda had a PhD in Marine Biology and had made a career out of making the science behind exhibitions digestible. She had worked on the scripts of any number of science exhibitions and had written a number of children's science books, notably 'Oceans' published by Dorling Kindersley.

Ian's opening gambit was to assert his view that we should aim The Deep not at 10-12 year olds (as had been our unspoken policy to date) but for the over 50s.

He argued that children would come anyway. The increasing leisure market and those more likely to be the decision makers and with disposable income were what the marketing people call either Grey Wolves in public, or Golden Zimmers in private. If The Deep were to be a heavily themed attraction, the over 50s would not come. The 'grey wolves' would, Ian maintained, want a conventional aquarium. For this, no exhibition designers were necessary. Real Life could deal with any modest 'dry side' required.

Given our experiences in Lisbon, the targeting of the over 50s and a move away from heavy theming made sense even if Ian's conclusion with regards exhibition designers didn't, and any ideas of white knuckle rides, large simulator rides etc. were never seriously considered again.

Next we considered a large format Audio Visual Show 3D, IMAX, 360° or 180° cinemas. Given the size of each of these formats, any decision to include them on our site would have to be made right at the beginning. Although a 180° format show continued to surface from time to time afterwards, the idea was generally dismissed due to the hardware costs of installing and maintaining such a specialist audio-visual show. We also had a watchful eye on running costs and the expense of renewing or commissioning our own films would make these difficult to refresh in later years.

In retrospect this was one of our better decisions. A number of attractions have struggled to attract the numbers necessary to cover the running costs of large-screen cinema formats, and whilst they work for some for others they have proved almost fatal.

Whilst we had made some progress on what we were not going to do, the story that we were going to tell was still no better defined than "a journey through time". Exactly how we were to make this a reality without access to extinct animals or a functioning time machine was fast becoming a bit of a road block. Whilst Giles and I had discussed it often, we had only ever managed to conclude that, where aquariums do tell stories (and that was rare), they almost always involved beginning in a mountain stream, before taking in coastal estuaries and finally heading into the open ocean. Only Natural History Museums ever dealt with the seas of the past, and it was beginning to feel like there was probably a good reason for this.

Ian suggested that instead of past, present and future the major theme should be the environment and the threats to the ocean's various eco-systems. Again, whilst this was generally accepted as part of the story we should tell, we were all concerned to avoid either preaching or, worse still, for our visitor attraction to become depressing. Giles made the point that many environmental issues had two sides and that to be scientifically robust we should deal with both, and cited the enriched eco-systems and white corals attracted to oil rigs. (Many years later we were to work with BP to collect these delicate White Corals in the North Sea as part of a study with London Zoo.)

I suggested that our theme could be a sort of inside out Noah's Ark with species inside protected from the threats which face them in the wild. Luckily the proposal was ignored!

Coherent stories proved much more difficult to come up with, unique stories almost impossible. Clearly most other aquariums whose agendas were more than making money dealt with their own local environment. Should we be the Aquarium of the North Sea? We dismissed this option quickly. We knew grey fish in brown water would not set us apart from most of the competition, but more importantly, we wanted to change the image of the City, to do that we needed to position The Deep and the City as an international city, not as a 'northern fishing port'. It was, as so often before, about being ambitious and taking a world view.

Our story would continue to develop in the months ahead but would only really coalesce some eighteen months before opening. In the meantime and in the absence of a story, we began considering what our star species might be. Perhaps a story could be built around that. Ian Cunningham suggested that commercially, porpoises would guarantee success. The meeting went quiet as others looked to me as if to say, well, you seem to be agreeing with him on everything else, you tell him!

"Won't that raise some environmental issues, keeping marine mammals in captivity is questionable to say the least." Ian warmed to his idea. "No, it's a sanctuary; we rescue sick or wounded animals and nurse them back to health."

"Are there enough wounded porpoises about?" I asked, visions of bandaged cetaceans, eye patches, limping back from a rumble, flashed through my mind.

"Dolphins are racists" Giles contributed unhelpfully. "They've been known to gang up and rape porpoises." Now I had images of skinhead Flippers, swastika tattoos on their dorsal fins, goading their mates – "Leave him Flipper he ain't worth it."

The meeting was quickly becoming surreal. "Thank you, Giles," I began," given that whilst I accept we may find the odd porpoise who needs counselling, I repeat: are there enough injured porpoises and if so, what happens when they get better?" Ian smiled, an evil smile, "Trust me, they don't get better!"

We decided to adjourn.

CHAPTER 16 WINTER 1998/99

CAMDEN LIBRARY

"Each new success only buys an admission ticket to a more difficult problem."
Henry Kissinger

By the end of the second meeting we still had our Natural History of the Sea theme which we had had from the outset. We had the name, The Deep, which by now was well known in the City and which we were beginning to be reluctant to change and we had some of the original ideas from Words and Ideas. It had to be said though, we had little else.

Time was by now pressing down on us like a Sumo wrestler on a third date. The design of the building had to begin now if we were to meet our programme and so the absence of a clear exhibition master plan was beginning to endanger the whole project. In London at Terry Farrell's offices we met again for another 2-day marathon. The architect had, in response to our previous meetings, begun to work up an initial concept plan for how the major tank would fit within the building. He had asked both MET Studios and Real Life Leisure for their minimum requirements and now Julian, Terry Farrell's lead architect on the project, was ready to reveal his findings and his initial sketch drawings.

Firstly Real Life Leisure's input showed a triangular building almost entirely filled by an enormous central tank leaving only narrow corridors down each side. Following our trip to Lisbon we had resolved to try and incorporate as big a central tank as possible but we also felt there should be some room left for customers! This proposal now being unveiled was, we were reminded, the minimum that Real Life Leisure and IAT required. As a counter, Julian then revealed the sketch incorporating MET Studios minimum requirement: this showed a tiny blue box in the centre of acres upon acres of dry exhibit galleries. "It's going to be another long day", I whispered to Giles.

Battle was soon joined again between our consultants, one in favour of 90% aquarium and 10% interactive, and the other in favour of, well, exactly the opposite.

The mood was changed when Terry Farrell joined us and began to share with us his initial thoughts on the interior feel of the building. To help explain he had bought along pictures of divers swimming amongst rock columns, shafts of sapphire light piercing the midnight recesses, highlighting the divers' rubber bodysuits. They were only pictures from magazines but they gave the first glimpse of what might be achievable if only we could find a way forward.

Terry spoke as he laid out the pictures on the table, "I have in mind a building integrated with its displays, forming part of them not merely housing them. Three dimensional spaces with views up and down reflecting the ocean itself." As he spoke he sketched a scribbled thing, landings in space, people on balconies, a house without stairs, without floors. It was only a sketch but it was inspiring.

At last we all had at least one theme we could agree on. The Deep would, where possible, not be a two dimensional journey, it would be three dimensional, and clearly this implied a journey from top to bottom as well. If the name was to remain 'The Deep' then visitors would expect to see the Deep Ocean, or at least an impression of it. A deep central tank then, and a descent, but from where and to where?

With everyone mentally exhausted the meeting broke up at about 3.30 pm. Tomorrow we would meet again and try and take the key decisions including the big one, big tank or little tank? Giles and I decided that as client we needed to provide more leadership to the design team, we needed to be clearer about what we wanted if we were to get the best out of them.

Like most Millennium Projects we were a virgin client, inexperienced in the ways of the creative process. We had heard of examples of where a single individual passionate about their subject had dictated to the design team every detail, resulting in an academically accurate but uninspiring exhibition.

As Director of Leisure I had learnt not to try and out-expert my experts; in a department covering everything from art galleries to crematoria it was impossible to be knowledgeable about installation art and the intricacies of the four phase burner! In any case it was so much more civilised to stay above the day-to-day details.

There had, of course, been times when I had inadvertently been drawn into the mire, like the time my crematorium manager had called me out of a meeting to explain that due to a mix up in the paperwork we had buried the wrong body in a newly dug family grave and that he wanted to know what we should say to the "right" family who had just arrived with their deceased! Or the time when I had taken my elderly Mother to the Council-run theatre to see an Al Jolson impersonator only to have him berate me mercilessly from the stage for having banned him from blacking up as part of his act. No, in general, the further I could stay away from the nitty gritty of such problems the better, so much less stressful to leave those with the knowledge to get on with the job and then to criticise them later with the power of hindsight enhanced where necessary with night vision goggles. This philosophy had always served me well and I saw no reason to change now.

For these reasons we had rather thought that we would set the general themes of an exhibition and then wait for our design team's creative juices to digest them, creating something original and exciting.

It was becoming clearer by the day however, that by trying to mediate between Real Life Leisure, MET Studios and the Architect we were failing to do the one thing that was our job ...to lead. With this in mind Giles and I stopped on our way back from Terry Farrell's studio to visit the British Library and to seek some inspiration, discovering to our surprise that you aren't actually allowed to look at books here, we finally stopped off at Camden Library and whilst Giles scoured the shelves for source material, I contacted my own office in Hull to get them to find out the dimensions of other aquariums' main tanks.

At 1.30 am that morning in my hotel room Giles and I finished our brief. The next morning at Terry Farrell's offices we presented our thoughts to the design team.

Firstly, we said, that although we were not just an aquarium we should aim to at least match the best in Britain. Our main tank however did not need to be as big as had been indicated by Real Life Leisure to achieve that, a tank somewhere between the two extremes that had so far been suggested would still give us the biggest tank in the UK and one of the biggest in Europe. Our dry exhibits should then be enough to ensure that we were both unique and that we offered a more educational and interesting day out than any other UK aquarium.

We told the meeting that The Deep was to be a journey through time, past, present and future. It being difficult to get hold of living plesiosaurs, most of the aquarium displays would therefore have to be in the middle part of the journey with the past and future sections concentrating more on the use of audio visual and interactives. The past however might include the possibility of a Mediterranean tank dressed with Greek columns and amphora, perhaps an Atlantis theme?

The Present Day aquarium exhibits would be arranged as a circumnavigation of the globe from equator to pole following the meridian line, which we had realised travelled almost through our site.

Next, a coral tank would be based around the reefs off the Gold Coast, close to Freetown, which had a close historical connection with Hull through William Wilberforce and the abolitionist movement. The coral tank would include gold doubloons and the ribs of an old outrigger.

Travelling further north the Northern Seas tank would include a pipeline, oilrig leg and industrial paraphernalia.

The story of the Present would conclude with the Polar seas.

Luckily, good taste prevailed and our ideas for some of the tackier theming were quickly removed although the industrial dressing to the Northern Seas remained and was built.

Jeremy argued that the Mediterranean as an ecosystem was not particularly rich and would add little to the overall displays and so this too was removed early on.

Our presentation was, to our genuine surprise warmly welcomed by everyone. Julian Topliss, the architect, said it was the best brief he had ever received from a client; although it must be said he was very young.

The discussion now moved on quickly to the question as to what the theme and depth of the main tank should be. This time the argument was between Ian and Jeremy. Ian, concerned with the availability and cost of replacement fish and no doubt with an interest in building something with which his own organisation felt comfortable, argued for a main tank that was 3 or 4 metres deep and with a temperate, North Sea theme, whilst Jeremy with greater international experience and a desire to show off the quality of his water treatment systems argued for a massive ten metre deep tank housing a real coral display which customers would enter via a moving walkway.

There were strengths in both ideas we felt. The Deep certainly needed to be seen as international. We were determined not to be seen as parochial, if we were to focus only on our own local ecosystems we would always be perceived as Hull's Aquarium and little more. We also had an almost obsessive desire to avoid what the Chairman always called grey fish in brown water, a display so common in domestic aquariums.

But a North Sea tank would surely be considerably cheaper to establish and maintain. A coral reef tank, of this scale, particularly one with real coral, seemed to threaten massive running costs in heating, lighting, fish and coral replacement as well as in technical and curatorial support, not to mention the problems of sourcing real coral, in an environmentally friendly way.

My first career was in Swimming Pool Management and whilst to-date this background had been of less use than a luminous sun dial, I did recall that after the cost of lifeguards (an expense I hoped to avoid at The Deep) the biggest cost was energy. The financial (and environmental) costs of heating a large body of water even by one degree centigrade were significant. Perhaps with conventionally sized aquarium tanks heating or cooling costs may not be as crucial but our main tank still dominated the plans pinned around the walls; in scale it was the equivalent of 3 Olympic swimming pools, hardly what most people would call a fish tank!

We asked at what temperature the main tank would settle at if no heating or cooling was used. Clearly heat would be lost from the surface of the tank and through the concrete walls and floor. But the water itself would act as a massive heat sink; it would absorb heat from the general heating in the building and heat would bleed into the water from the pumps and water treatment processes. The answer was 24 degrees centigrade and so that became the temperature of the main display, 24 degrees translated as a warm water open ocean environment.

In retrospect we had initially misunderstood the role of our consultants, or more accurately our own role as clients. They were there to comment, assist, even act as devil's advocate (not to be confused with the Devil's Advokaat, which our mythological helper had discovered gave you one hell of a hangover), but we had an important role too; we had to know what we wanted; now we did!

Our decision regarding the subject matter of the main tank was not only a turning point in the evolution of the displays; it was also a turning point in our ambition and, in reality, about the balance of power in the project. If, as a client, we continued to go against our commercial partners' wishes (as we had with our decision on the main tank), if we continued to follow our ambitions, then our fear was that our private sector partner might conclude that they could no longer make an adequate return and that they too would withdraw from the project. Without an operator we would have no one to share any revenue risk. On the other hand, we had no guarantee that Real Life Leisure would ever have been willing to accept a share of the risk in any case and if they were allowed to veto this decision where would that leave us in all the similar debates which would surely follow?

Once back in Hull I felt this was one decision I needed some guidance on, if only to share the blame if this second and very delicate commercial partnership was to flounder.

Whilst I knew what the Chairman's view would be (he would not compromise his vision to pacify a partner with whom we still had no long term relationship), we nevertheless discussed the situation we were in. The Council's support had almost always been conditional upon us having a private partner confident enough to share the risks. Now the price of that private sector support was developing into a downgrading of our, and the city's, growing ambitions for The Deep. We asked to see the Council's Chief Executive, Ian Crookham and Leader Councillor Pat Doyle.

The meeting, when it came a few days later, could not have been more positive and helpful to our position. We explained the position and the choices before us. Pat and Ian explored further, education being Pat's major concern, and before long the instruction was given. Build us what the City needs, not what Real Life Leisure wants.

Pat and Ian's logic was clear; if The Deep achieves its educational, image and regeneration agendas then these would justify the Council's support alone. Whilst we should always consider carefully the revenue implications of any decision we make and whilst no promises were given or asked for, it was clear that, if the worst happened, a Council subsidy for a resource which helped push Hull off the bottom of the education league tables would be justifiable; a subsidy to a Sea Life competitor would not be.

Armed with this we discussed the issue at our next Shadow Board. Whilst the City's view was powerful, it was the independent view of the Trustees that now counted most. It proved to be one of many times when the Trustees would err on the side of quality, a strategy which never proved misplaced. Professor Kopp summed it up: "We are meant to be The Deep not the murky shallows!"

With this we went to the next meeting of the consultants well-armed. We would not have a massive coral tank, not for reasons of cost but because corals, even artificial ones, have to be viewed close up; they are as we put it "painted with a fine brush." We would have an open coral lagoon tank, but our main tank would be pelagic or warm water Open Ocean it would be ten metres deep and this depth would be one of the projects unique attributes. From that day the name "The Deep" was never questioned again.

This new-found confidence from their client appeared to both surprise and please the design team. Rather than walking off the project, even Ian seemed to begin to understand and accept our vision better.

With the tank size and temperature agreed we quickly moved onto choosing which species to display. The choice of species to be displayed seemed on the face of it to be several years ahead of schedule; it felt like we were choosing the colour of the carpets before the walls were designed. In fact, it was now clear that choosing the species for display was a critical decision. Firstly they would have to live naturally at 24 degrees but more than that their needs would inform the ideal shape and size for the tank as well as its water treatment requirements. Jeremy, having accepted the position with the main tank, proposed a Manta Ray as our star species. Reluctantly given the beauty of these creatures, the idea was discarded simply because, whilst our new tank was big, it was not, could never be, that big! Without enough knowledge of specific species therefore we simply listed the body shapes we required – sharks, rays, eels, shoaling fish.

We were now finding some fixed reference points in the project, we knew the building would be 3-sided to fit the site, it would be built around a single large tank housing warm water pelagic species, and that other tanks would include Polar, North Sea and Coral. However, we still felt that the aquarium displays were nothing new. We had not yet found a way of breaking through what Giles called the glass ceiling of imagination which even the best aquariums appeared to have reached.

True we had not yet explored the possibilities of the dry exhibitory, but we knew that The Deep must be more than just another aquarium if it were to attract sufficient visitors. The City needed something that had never been done before. Other aquariums competed by providing bigger tanks, or more tanks, both of which were beyond our budget; we needed to find a way of using the available technology to make ours different. To quote someone famous," We didn't have the money so we had to think!"

There are stories about bands of monkeys on different sides of an island who never contact each other and yet both appear to have discovered how to use rocks to open shell-fish within days of each other. Perhaps there is some involuntary telepathy between individuals or perhaps it's just as simple as individuals drawing the same conclusions from the information supplied. Some may even perhaps, with some justification, say that success has many fathers, failure is an orphan. Whatever the reasons, from wherever it came, the answer was to add a scenic lift that would rise through the main tank. The idea was to have a final ride, a final wow which would be unique and exciting without scaring the over 50s. Initially David Gemmell wanted it to rise in the dead centre in the tank, but this would have meant that the lift would lack any physical means of support. Julian rather apologetically explained that this would not only be against building regulations but also went against the laws of the known universe!

Against such evidence eventually even David compromised: we would have 2 x 180° scenic lifts, supported by the tank wall. Whilst we were pleased with the idea it was only some months later that we were to discover that even this more prosaic solution would be unique in the world.

Later still, much later, ten years later to be precise, the newspaper, America Today, pronounced our lift ride the best lift in the world beating the Empire State Building and the Eiffel tower, amongst others.

It was now time to try and pull all of these pieces together into some coherent whole, to blend the exhibition interiors with the still evolving building. It was now up to MET Studios and Terry Farrell's to work together to develop the plan further.

Their initial report when it came was presented to the design team and then the full Shadow Board. It showed an initial gallery space which was dark and theatrical. A winding causeway curled its way into and around the space. Waterfalls provided vertical axis, water cascaded down through the building. A giant globe hung in the middle of this space projected onto which images showed the fiery planet at its birth on one side and the blue planet of today on its reverse.

Ice comets rifled from the abyss of space towards the embryo earth bringing with them the water that would form the oceans. The walkway was of glass, the end wall of rock, with fossils showing creatures from the ocean's distant past. The introduction dealt with, the concept drawings then showed the aquarium displays which became dominant.

An acrylic walled escalator took the visitor down from coral lagoon through a coral wall. The main tank was followed by the North Sea area. Open to the elements the North Sea tank also displayed diving birds; touch pools, study areas and an outside gallery which was linked to a roof walkway.

The Polar gallery incorporated an ice wall and the Deep theatre had become a more modest version of a 180° AV show. Finally the two underwater lifts returned the visitor to the third floor shop and cafeteria.

The whole experience was housed in the most amazing building. Crystalline in form it shot from the ground like a thousand shards of glass. Its outward sloping walls made it look more like Superman's Fortress of solitude than an aquarium. It was stunning, and even though we realised it was only conceptual it took our breath away, and was a quantum jump from our original vision.

The architect commissioned a model and as soon as it was finished we launched the building to a packed audience appropriately at the Ferens Art Gallery. The press loved it as did everyone else; it was truly a modern icon.

As the audience began to leave the Gallery, Neil, Giles and I were sought out by Robert Haskins from Government Office, the head guy when it came to the various European grants we were seeking and which we still needed to match with the Millennium grant.

Originally when we had approach Robert he was, let's just say, rigorous in his interrogation of the business case.

Having perhaps slightly overcooked my presentation to him on the financial viability of The Deep, I remember him saying that if it was that good an idea I should spend my own money on it. I nearly replied that if I had had £40 million I wouldn't be sitting with him in a dingy office in Leeds on a cold Tuesday morning.... but I wisely resisted.

However, Robert had been a great supporter for some time now and he advised Neil and me to get the European bid documents in immediately. It appeared that a number of bids which Government office had been expecting to receive had fallen by the way side and a window had opened up, but only if we moved quickly. Giles wanted more time to refine the arguments but we decided there and then to take Roger's advice. We would send in the bid pretty much as it stood.

The conversation with Robert had been the most positive news we had had for some time on the European front and was a big step towards us securing the next biggest tranche of funding.

With everyone now having left the Gallery I stood alone and looked again at the model of Terry Farrell's concept aquarium. Whilst it was indeed stunning, we were already beginning to understand the limits of even our budget and I couldn't help thinking that if such a building was possible for a little under £40 million why weren't there more of them around? Disney regularly spends more than our entire budget on a single theme park ride, could our relatively meagre budgets really stretch to this amazing vision?

CHAPTER 17　　　　　　　　　　　　　　　　SPRING 1999

HMS SINKING SHIP

"Sometimes I get the feeling that the whole world is against me, but deep down I know that's not true. Some of the smaller countries are neutral."
Robert Orben

As is always the case when one prepares oneself for the unexpected, something else happens.

The Lucky Little Devil crouched over his toilet groaning and resting his clammy brow on his forearms. He was much too young for clubbing it. Just a few beers he had thought. What could be the harm in that? And he was right at least for a while. The club had been both loud and dark and being both quiet and invisible he had finally felt at home. In fact he was convinced that some of the more energetic youngsters there, those with the vacant expressions, did actually see him. At least they acknowledged him and one tall thin girl had begun to chat him up.

Then it had all started to go wrong, he'd been O.K. with all six types of beer that the club sold, and he'd enjoyed the perfumed taste of the three different gins on offer, but the Advokaat had tasted a bit slimy as if some idiot had mixed brandy with eggs or something! But still he was convinced it hadn't been that that had made him ill. No, it seemed clear to him that it was the fizzy Perrier stuff that had made him ill, there ought to be a law against it, a warning on the label – Danger, this stuff should not be mixed with beer, gin and Advokaat, he thought.

There was no way he could get to work this morning, he'd phone up and tell them he had the flu.

With the Lucky Devil out of commission, the project reverted to type! The Millennium commission had insisted that the team take a day out to discuss what risks might exist and how we might plan to minimise them; it seemed wise enough and I was about to find out just how wise.

As with so many problems on the project, this one began with a phone call and also like so many problems, Keith German, the project manager, was the bearer of the bad news.

"This risk management workshop in Doncaster tomorrow, can you get here a bit earlier? We've got a bit of a problem with the costs for the building." And so it was that at 7.30 am in a dreary Doncaster hotel reception I was told that the initial costing for the building was £5 million over our budget. The building, albeit still in concept form, which we had launched publicly and to such acclaim, only weeks before, was, it transpired, almost impossible to construct, at least not with technology currently available on Planet Earth.

The sloping walls were at such an angle that builders didn't know if they were walls or floors, and so with a loud sucking of teeth, had basically given us the "Dear oh dear, that's gonna cost you that is gov'nor" gambit.

I had foolishly assumed that some part of an architect's brief was to conceive to a budget, but when you give an architect of the quality of Terry Farrell the brief to build you an icon, you get vision first and budget second. Time would of course prove Terry right. Without the vision, an icon would be impossible; with one, the challenge became to deliver as close to the vision as possible. Not surprisingly, I was somewhat distracted when the real risk management meeting began later.

We spent the morning discussing what risks there were to the project with the Millennium Commission staff. We brainstormed potential problems and managed to cover an entire wall of the conference room with them, and that was without the one that remained unspoken and undocumented, the big one, the one which would have read: we are so far from having a building design which we can afford that we are in effect about to start the building design afresh for a third time.

Whilst we waited for the architect to do the impossible and to create a stunning icon building from scratch in a few months for less than £40 million we had no option but to continue with the other aspects of the project design, in the hope that the building would soon catch up. So several weeks later at a meeting in the architect's London offices to discuss the tank design I was called out of the meeting to be presented with the latest elevations of the building. Over the preceding weeks the building's angled walls had become only half as sloping, it had lost 2 metres in width and its entire shop and entrance area had disappeared. Its crevasses had been trimmed and then filled and its characteristic glass nose cone was gone, becoming instead a 'sea cave' and still, I was told, the building remained over our budget.

Out went the sea birds, the exterior tanks and the shop area. Some, although precious few, of the changes to be fair turned out to be improvements; for example, we lost one of our two scenic lifts and replaced it with a scenic staircase allowing visitors two different experiences and providing those who felt uncomfortable in lifts with an alternative exit route.

But it was the exterior changes that made my heart sink.

As I listened to a most articulate and intelligent presentation of the new building design, my mind kept repeating, oh my god it's a sinking ship!

It was all there: the original thrusting arrowhead had somehow become the bow of a ship slowly sinking below the waves. The steel-plate cladding, once part of a new geological metaphor, now spoke simply of ship's plate. Where once the diamond crystalline nose cone had proclaimed Hull's confidence to the world, there was now a ship's bridge, its dark recesses no doubt hiding this ship's incompetent look-out.

I had heard once that the look-out on the Titanic had come from Hull. Now I imagined I could see him squinting short-sightedly from inside the 'bridge' saying "Is it me or has it suddenly turned chilly?" as an iceberg the size of Belgium glides towards him.

The human brain loves patterns. We see patterns everywhere, even when they don't exist, and if you give a brain 2 or 3 visual clues that say, for example, 'face', it will place the missing features in for itself. Once my brain had said 'ship' it then proceeded to read every other detail as part of that picture. Windows became portholes, lift shafts became funnels and even the irregular concrete base became the ocean's waves, rising to consume HMS Deep. And yet, this 'Millennium Titanic' for all its problems was still over budget and all the time the design stage was eating into both our money and our time.

I could feel the project sliding towards disaster. We were now on our third design and as far as the building was concerned we might as well be starting from scratch. We were haemorrhaging money and time and we weren't past the start line yet.

The architect, indeed the project, needed some decisions and fast. I promised to take the visuals back to Hull. Perhaps it was me; perhaps others would not see the ship. I managed to get an urgent appointment to see the Chief Executive and the Leader and, recalling snippets of the architect's arguments I tried my best to convince them of its merits, unsuccessfully. I called an emergency Shadow Board meeting and this time insisted that someone from Farrell's come to present it. An architect duly arrived and presented the new visuals as best he could.

The Board members, who had listened politely to the presentation were unanimous: it was a ship, a sinking ship, worse still, a sinking container ship. The Deputy Chair of our Board, John Parkes, delivered the killer blow, the building, he said, was now "Ordinary". Ugly, the architect present could have sold to Terry Farrell as "controversial" but now he would have to report, the client thought it ordinary!

Like a Middle East peace envoy my next mission was back to London to see Terry Farrell to convey the feelings of the Board, the Council and City Vision.

Terry is, unlike the reputation given to signature architects by those with more envy than talent, one of the least arrogant men I know. His skill, at least one of his skills, is simply listening. There is no denying that he was shocked by the negative reaction, he was convinced that the building as designed would be an icon, it would be dramatic and unique. He had not read it as a ship, nor had anyone in his practice. But then their daily lives were not punctuated by the Humber river traffic or a culture of sea and ship. He tried once again to crystallise his thought processes.

This wasn't a ship, he said. It was geological; he had, he explained, become fascinated by the metaphor, a landscape eroded by time, weathered into new original shapes, shapes that spoke of antiquity and of natural decay, and then it struck me," That was the problem", I said. "Hull doesn't want decay, we've been there and we are changing. The Deep was meant to represent a new landscape for Hull, Geological yes, but a new escarpment which rose from the ground yesterday not a million years ago."

It was a remark made almost in frustration but, finally, we had provided Terry with a real brief for our icon. Terry immediately began to explore and unwrap the thought, giving it a power I had never intended but was happy to claim credit for. Terry agreed to rework the exteriors and to present his new Deep mark 3 to the Board in just two weeks' time. These would have to be acceptable to City Vision the City Council and the Board or the whole project may have to be cancelled. If he couldn't do it we would seriously have to ask if it were now even possible to complete the project on time and on budget. Time had now run out.

With our Chair and deputy's (John Parkes') approval I invited all the key players to Terry's presentation at the Guildhall. Only if everyone agreed would we have the confidence to move forward and for that we would need a fabulous building and not a little luck.

Once again when our need was greatest we were given both. Terry's new building was clean, proud and stunning. Smiles spread around the room. Terry began presenting his new design but there was really no need; to quote Renee Zellweger, "he had us at Hello"!

By chamfering off the point of the building Terry had been able to keep the thrusting feel and had also been able to reduce the slope of the sides to a more manageable and affordable angle. Gone were the round port hole windows to be replaced by random squares which gave the impression of jewels set in the stone. We had lost the exterior bird exhibit and a totally impractical external entry lift. Whilst the eastern aspect admittedly provided the least successful, rather stumpy view, the southern and western views were exactly what we had hoped for.

The problem was, though, that despite this major surgery we still believed that this new building would remain significantly over budget, In the time available, it had been impossible for Gleeds, our quantity surveyors, to provide an accurate cost for Terry's new designs; certainly we had good reason to believe that the simplified lines and reduced angles would have a significant effect but we had no more accurate costing than those provided by the architect himself. For all of TFP's design skills, however, asking them for cost advice was a bit like asking an alcoholic how much he thought he drank in a week; they would both give you what they thought was an honest answer but neither were really best placed to do so.

Nevertheless, we had to go with the best figure we had and that was that we would need an additional £1.7m; Coincidentally we were already nursing a £1.7m funding gap and without some comfort the Shadow Board could not agree to spend money it didn't have.....twice!

By presenting the new design and costs openly to the various stakeholders the decision was clear and their support underscored. No doubt it helped that, only a few months earlier the City's financial situation, at least in terms of capital, had been transformed by the sale of 50% of its Kingston Communications shares. The deal had brought the Council £250m but more importantly the rise and rise of telecommunications shares began to push the Council's remaining shareholding to £300, £500, £800 million and then for a few golden weeks to a staggering one billion pounds.

The Council agreed to provide its first serious capital contribution to the project in March 1999 by releasing £1.7million to cover the additional costs of the new building. The Council was adamant that this was not a grant to bail out The Deep but it was a grant to ensure quality and this is exactly what it did.

With the additional grant, the project seemed to be achievable again if not exactly in robust financial health. Of course even if we were to receive all of the grants we had applied for we would still have our original funding gap of £1.7million to fill, but the various European bids were proceeding calmly through the system and we began to receive informal reassurances about them. We still had a number of other funding opportunities to investigate and our level of contingencies remained good.

So we now had an iconic design and most, if not all, of the funding in place. We had a fabulous site, public support, a professional consultancy team in place, a construction programme which they had all signed up to and even an embryonic organisation capable of taking the project through to completion ...or so we thought.

CHAPTER 18   SUMMER 1999

CONTRACT KILLING

"There are some things you learn best in calm and some in storm."

Willa Cather

Finally, we had a building and an exhibition concept that we knew would provide us with the icon that we wanted, perhaps our lucky Devil was back on our case after all. Of course all of these additional design phases must have had a cost - we just weren't very sure yet what that had been.

We were told that whilst it was still possible to deliver the building by the end of 2001, the room for error had now become very narrow. The Millennium Commission had, given their name, not unreasonably, insisted that their projects should be completed by the end of the millennium year which contrary to public opinion was actually 2001. Just as importantly our second major funder the European Union (which by now had agreed our funding requests) wanted its money spent by the end of that same year and had been known to reclaim funds if their timescales were missed.

Keith German our project manager looked again at the programme and presented the Shadow Board with a stark choice.

In short, we could still make the target date providing that we opted for a contract which allowed us to begin letting key contracts and even starting construction work before the architects had worked through the final details on the building. In reality this meant starting to build the building without the finished plans being available. Whilst scary, this was apparently by no means unknown in the building trade and was a well-known tactic for speeding a contract to conclusion. Keith pointed out that there were additional risks to such a course of action, but in reality the Board had little or no choice. It would either accept a greater risk in the structure of contracts let or it would have to go back to its two major funders and inform them that it could not deliver the project in the timescale expected. Although by now the funding had been agreed it had not yet been paid and this would in effect have killed the project. The Board ended on quite a positive note: it seems strange looking back now but the biggest problem we felt we faced at this point was confidence. Whilst everything now looked to be in place our delicately assembled house of cards could still collapse at any time. We hadn't started work on site and, should there be a change of policy from the Government, the Millennium Commission, Europe, or one of so many other agencies The Deep could still be cancelled and filed away like so many other aborted projects. We needed to get builders on site and to quite literally begin to make The Deep concrete. This form of contract would allow that to happen. It was called a management contract, but it was the same use of words which allows the world's most tyrannical regimes call themselves The Democratic Republic of.....

In brief, this meant that whereas in a conventional building project you would

1. Design the building
2. Build the building

In a management contract the aim is for the detailed design to run in parallel with the construction, a sort of just in time process. Put simply, we needed the architect to remain at least one step ahead of the builders. If, for whatever reason, the design began to fall behind we would have expensive plant and people standing around consuming money.

Management contracts seem to work best where the risks and complexity in the construction process are low or at least known. In our case we had a number of complications which included the fact that the site had been marinating for 50 years in a toxic soup of dangerous chemicals including Arsenic, Cadmium and enough methane bubbles to turn the site into a giant explosive Aero bar!

Secondly, we had a signature architect and a liberal portion of uncertainty inherent in building a novel, indeed unique building. We had a quantity surveyor still trying to get a handle on its cost, and we had a virgin client. Together these problems (as well as others) gave us all the ingredients to create the building project from Hell.

Whilst the management contract reassured the Millennium Commission and allowed the project to proceed, it meant that from now on any late revisions would not involve moving lines on a drawing but moving concrete on site. This opened the possibility that we would be reworking the building every time one plan didn't quite fit with the one before.

Still we had no choice, and we were still on an optimistic high. We had faced problems before and we had overcome them; whatever the problems in the future we would navigate our way through them. After all, there was every chance we would get it right first time. As long as luck stayed with us!

The exhibition master planners, MET Studios, had been developing there thinking now for some time and had done some great work. They had explained that we had three possible ways to structure the exhibition.

Firstly we could have a pulsed exhibition. This would have entailed gathering small groups of visitors together at the beginning and then taking them, as a group, into a series of rooms, or experiences. This was the system used in some of the Pavilions in Lisbon and was used during the early parts of the exhibition at our sister Millennium Project, Dynamic Earth in Edinburgh. This system literally pulsed visitors around the exhibition at set intervals, allowing for films or presentations to have clearly defined starts and finishes. As we had seen in Lisbon, however, such pulsing can be inflexible during busy periods, causing long queues and yet also requires a high level of staffing as it is often proves necessary to guide groups from the end of one part of the exhibition to the start of the next.

A second possibility was to have a much more free-form structure, like that used in most traditional museums. Here visitors enter and are then free to explore the story as they see fit. There may be some flow lines subtly encouraged by way of signage and narrative, but essentially the space allows visitors maximum freedom but provides minimal guidance and can create a weak sense of narrative. The lack of a clear start and finish can also encourage visitors to stay all day, reducing capacity during peak periods.

The third possibility was to have a clearly defined route around the exhibition, whilst still allowing visitors to both retrace their steps if they so wished as well as allowing individuals to experience the exhibition at their own pace.

Given our storyline MET Studios felt that the third option would be preferable as it would also lend itself better to us being able to achieve the feeling of being in a 3-dimensional space. By structuring the exhibition using a series of suspended walkways we could achieve the feeling of descent through the water. These ramps would be both dramatic and practical as they would create a natural flow to the visitor experience, taking people from beginning to end and allowing us to develop a clear storyline.

Visitor attractions are extremely seasonal and dependent on school holidays. An attraction that can't cope on a Bank Holiday Monday may be lucky to get 50 visitors on the following Tuesday. This means that it is important to be able to maximise usage on busy days. With the ramped approach we thought that we would be better able to cope with large numbers at peak times whilst not being burdened with excessive staffing costs during the much quieter days.

It was for all these reasons that we went with option 3. We were delighted with MET's concept of the descending ramps; they would gently encourage visitors onwards through a linear story until they eventually reached the exit, but without actually restricting users from retracing their steps if they wanted to. It was a strategy which depended to a great extent on encouraging visitors to discover what lies around the next corner and on making each area hold visitors for a similar length of time. It was a big step forward and we now had an internal architecture as exciting as the external one onto which we could start to build.

The story of a journey through time and depth was now well accepted and with the ideas we had liberated from our Lisbon trip we felt we could at last start to populate the exhibition with specific displays.

But now, MET Studios, our exhibition master planners, began to give use cause for concern. We had been pleased with their early work and we were beginning to see the bones of a successful exhibition emerging. Almost literally as one of the first ideas to take its place was the fossil wall, an idea which had been triggered by seeing a series of projected images of fossils on a wall in the Lisbon Ocean Pavilion. For some reason this sparked a discussion about how all fossils are displayed in two dimensions and lack any sense of drama. We wanted to see the skeletons of these long-dead creatures exposed in such a way as if they were bursting from the rock in which they had been imprisoned, and MET's fossil wall gave us just that.

However, whilst we had a number of strong parts of the exhibition, MET seemed to want to move on to detailed designs before we had every area as strong as we wanted. They seemed reluctant to focus on the weak areas as we had asked. We knew we needed a final wow and felt that that was now in place with the Scenic lift but we were unwilling to accept that any part of the exhibition would simply be a corridor or a ramp between exhibits or indeed that any part of The Deep exhibition would be less than it could be. It was against this background that Alex, from MET Studios, then informed us of the financial difficulties his company was facing, due to some bad Middle Eastern debts. He outlined his plan for avoiding bankruptcy and he outlined the reasons behind his current position. Whilst none of this seemed Alex's fault we were in no position to wait until his company went through a difficult and time-consuming restructuring. MET Studios had reached the end of their initial contract with us and we felt we had little choice but to advertise for other companies to take MET's concept on and to complete the last detailed phase of the exhibition design.

There had been some constructive conflict between the architect and the exhibition designers which, given our desire for an integrated exhibition, was perhaps unavoidable. Terry Farrell and Partners suggested that they should also have a role in the design of the exhibitions and produced a proposal in partnership with a new company of designers.

Whilst TFP failed to make the argument that both contracts should in effect be awarded to them nevertheless, they had impressed on us the advantages to be gained from a collaborative atmosphere between designer and architect. We were keen therefore to ensure that any exhibition designer appointed would be open enough to work collaboratively. Perhaps more than anything we sought enthusiasm for the task and an ability to work as part of a wider team.

We appointed John Czarky (pronounced Sharky..... yeah I know!) Associates to take the exhibition design forward. John was tall, slim and greying; although originally a sculptor, John and his team also showed an impressive grasp of the need to structure the creative process in order to achieve programme milestones. To begin the work, John proposed a study trip to view what is generally considered to be one the best aquariums in the world, in Monterey Bay, California. The plan was to stop off in New York and visit the American Museum of Natural History to view the only black smoker in captivity. Black smokers, or hydro-thermal vents, have only relatively recently been discovered in the deep ocean trenches. Massive chimney-like vents in the ocean floor, black smokers, as their name implies, bellow endless streams of chemically rich water and gas into the oceans and play host to the only ecosystem on earth which owes nothing to the sun. As such they could have been the place where life on earth began. They were clearly important to our story and to see one and perhaps cadge a sample would be invaluable.

The Shadow Board agreed that David, Giles and I should go. We were to be joined, at their own expense, by Keith German and by John Czarky, Andrew Wood-Walker from our new exhibition designers. Whilst we all felt the trip was important we were also aware that with our current funding gap it may cause some criticism. Luckily, Rollitts, our Solicitors, offered to sponsor the trip and so the arrangements were made.

▲ Plate 1

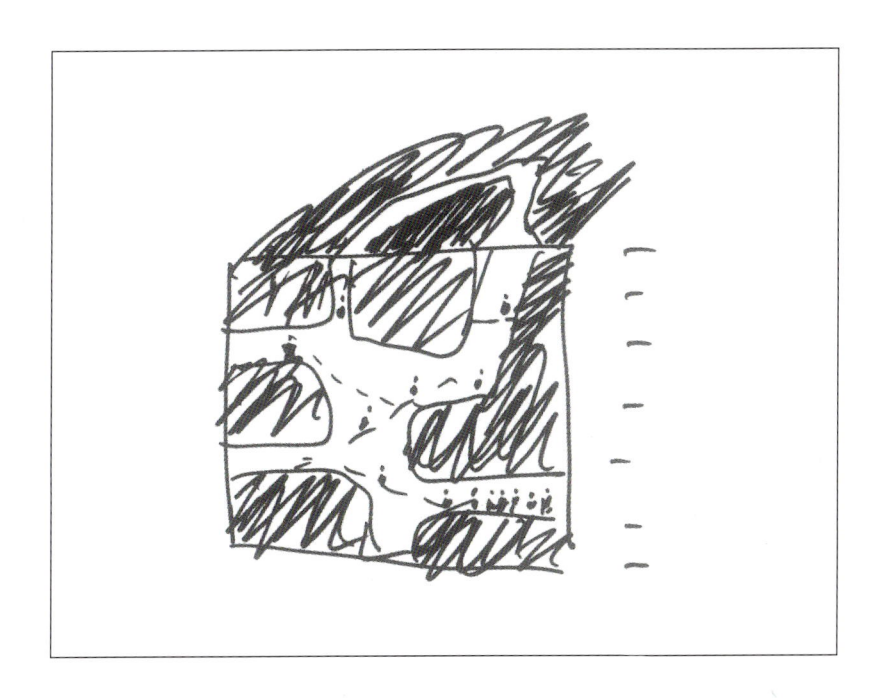

▲ Plate 2

▼ Plate 3

▲ Plate 4

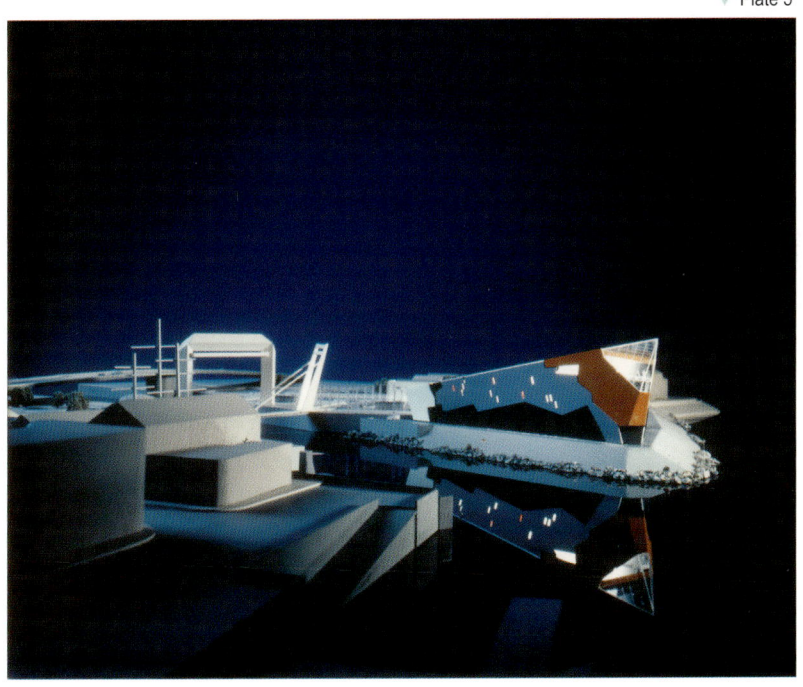

▼ Plate 5

▲ Plate 6

▲ Plate 7

▲ Plate 8

▲ Plate 9

▼ Plate 10

▲ Plate 11

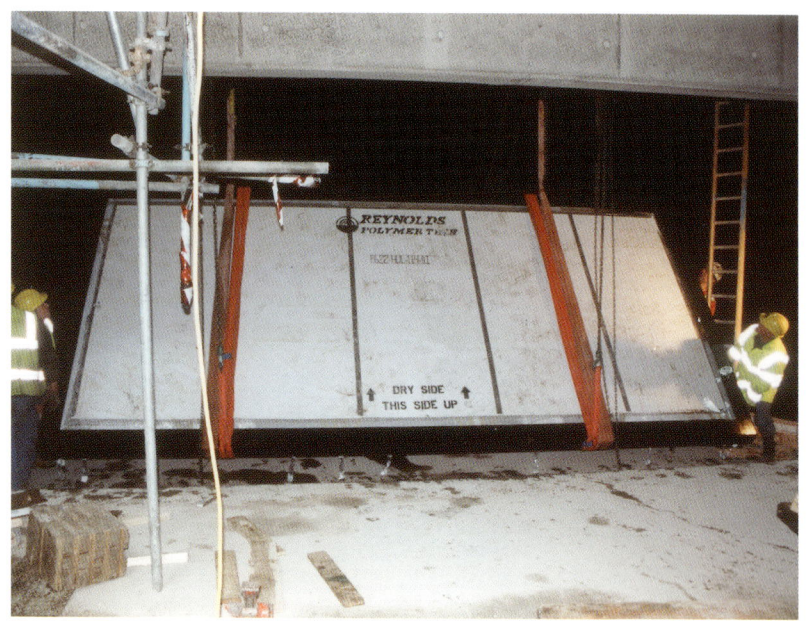

▼ Plate 12

▲ Plate 13

Plate 14

▲ Plate 15

▲ Plate 16

CHAPTER 19   AUTUMN 1999

OSWALD T. HALL

"It is a good thing for an uneducated man to read books of quotations."
Winston Churchill

As we prepared for our trip, everything about the project seemed to be in a state of change. With all the paperwork required to establish a more formal Board of Trustees now in place Tony Hunt joined the Board as did Trevor Boanus (pronounced Bonus). I had met Trevor only weeks earlier when we had discovered that the plans for our vital new bridge had already hit a major snag. As the lawyers scratched through the details of the proposed landing site for the bridge they had discovered that Trevor, a local business man, owned what amounted to a ransom strip of land which would prevent the bridge, and possibly therefore the whole project, from proceeding. I agreed with Ian Crookham that I should ask to see the owner Trevor, and see how difficult he would be. Trevor Boanus owned much of the land on the river bank opposite The Deep, as well as a range of other successful businesses. He now found himself in a position to potentially stop the project, or at least to get a really good price for his land.

Trevor is a big man, tall and broad, he sat at his board table with his equally big son Stuart; clearly, I thought, if this was to develop into a fist fight I would be lucky to get out alive!

I need not have worried. Although clearly no friend of the Council, or more accurately, of unnecessary Council bureaucracy, Trevor had been keeping up to date with our progress and despite my oversight in not having involved such a key player earlier, he was already a supporter. Trevor turned out to be a big man in both senses as he readily agreed to give us the access we needed at no cost, and later went on to be one of our biggest sponsors and one of our best friends.

Tony Hunt however, I had never met before. Tony had been a senior engineer with BP and, with the probable exception of Jack Brignall, perhaps had the most experience of all the Board members with construction and engineering. Like Mike Killoran, Tony had an enthusiasm and a plain-speaking way which was always welcome.

Tony was to more than play his part later, and again was to become one of our greatest advocates and friends.

Tony and Trevor gelled with the members of the shadow Board immediately. Now we had local politicians, academics and business leaders all together on the formal Board and the early signs were good.

If the Board was evolving, so was the design, as both the plans for the Business Centre and The Deep itself began to gather pace.

Giles became more and more concerned that whilst we now had some more construction experience on the Board we still lacked it amongst the staff of EMIH, which by now consisted of himself, Neil Porteus on Finance, Louise Kirby with Diane Porter providing admin support, and Linda Martin dealing with PR.

Whilst I remained interested in anything which looked fun, exhibitions, marketing etc., I had been withdrawing from the project in order to let the newly formed Board, together with Giles, its new Company Secretary, find their feet. It was clear that my own experience in major construction projects was limited, although a better word might be non-existent and that Giles was right: as a group we were to building what the Teletubbies were to heavy engineering. We had by now appointed Bovis as the main contractor and BDP were busy with the drawing up of tender documents for everything from flood defences to roofing contractors, but the staff of EMIH still seemed strangely distant from the process.

On a day-to-day basis the project was managed, for want of a more appropriate word, through a series of monthly project team meetings chaired by Keith German of BDP. There was no denying that they were indeed meetings, at least on a physical if not intellectual level, but the word "team" was not something that could accurately be applied to them. It soon became clear that the obvious pressures of time and money which the delays had caused, as well as the continuing absence of sufficiently developed plans, were combining to send each consultant running for excuses rather than focusing on solving problems. Again it felt like we would have to do what we had done over the impasse on the initial design and become more proactive as a client.

But this time it would have to be Giles that took the lead. I had, not for the first time, been told to come away from the project and let the new Board find their own way.

Giles though had grown in stature and there was a new confidence about him, which could be traced directly back to the appointment of a new Vice Chancellor at the University.

David Dilks had stepped down and had been replaced by David Drewry, an ex-head of the British Antarctic Survey. This David was a geographer at heart and immediately threw his weight behind our work. Trevor Newsom left the University and an immediate review was ordered as to whether Jack Hardisty's computer-based Humber Observatory remained the right partner for us. The University's research role at The Deep quickly changed and it was decided that they would instead build a flume tank capable of modelling real estuarine environments. Professor Kopp, also now on the Board, was given the lead role.

Giles was encouraged to do everything he could to help deliver The Deep. Whilst he had always done so this newly found unambiguous direction and authority allowed him considerable freedom. Giles used this to press for the appointment of a Chief Executive who could lead the project full time and would have experience in the construction business. For my part, I was happy to take a lesser role; one of the regular re-organisations in the Council was nearing its climax and my Leisure Department looked like being improved beyond repair by the consultants' recommendations. My self-preservation instincts led me to believe that I should either be spending more time in my Department, or I would be spending more time with my family!

The Board took some weeks to be convinced by Giles that there was a role for another construction expert. They felt, not unreasonably, that BDP were already meant to be acting as our project managers. Giles, though, was closer to the action, and he had become wary of the role that BDP in general and Keith in particular were fulfilling. Keith and Giles's relationship was becoming more and more difficult and at times was quite adversarial. Although I am sure that they might disagree, it seems obvious now that individual consultants do not work for clients in the same way as "normal" employees do. They work for their own organisations. Thus Giles felt that Keith's first loyalty was to BDP. The Deep needed someone who would unambiguously represent us. A few weeks later the Board agreed to appoint a full-time Chief Executive and the post was advertised.

One candidate stood out immediately, Oswald T. Hall OBE; ex-military Ossie had built projects around the world not least in Northern Ireland and most recently in Hong

Kong. He was well known locally, being from a long- established Hull family and came across with all the energy and enthusiasm which (present company excluded) we were beginning to see as an essential pre-requisite for an EMIH employee.

Ossie offered to work for nothing and although we didn't take him at his word, it seemed a good omen. In looks, temperament and indeed background Ossie was almost a caricature of a British Military Officer. Excellent company socially, he nevertheless sent shock waves around the rest of the team, most of whom had been brought up in either academia or local government. Although Ossie had no knowledge of operational leisure management, that was not seen as a problem as we all still expected to let a management contract to a commercial operator and thus Ossie's role was always going to be somewhat short term.

Ossie also bought with him a peculiar vocabulary, which the rest of the team found amusing but almost impossible to follow. It was a sort of cross between British military jargon and nineteenth-century colonial. I remember Linda, our Public Relations Officer, thinking that a "Pooh trap" was some form of camouflaged pit found in the Hundred Acre Wood until Giles explained its true meaning (a situation or problem to be avoided). Ossie's vocabulary was so rich that, when Ossie was out of his office at a "Fat Boys' Dinner" (business lunch), the team would gather around the bell at reception whilst Giles hosted an impromptu game of Call My Bluff with contestants describing three different meanings to each "Ossieism".

Ossie immediately began to get a better grip on the consultant's team than I had had, and the client at last started to lead the monthly team meetings. Having some experience of construction he was less reliant on Keith and was better placed to drill down into the details. Of course this didn't make him the most popular of additions to the team, which didn't seem to bother him in the slightest.

CHAPTER 20   WINTER 1999/2000

CALIFORNIA DREAMING

"Everything is deemed possible except that which is impossible"
California Civil Code 1597

At last the day arrived for our mission to Monterey Bay and at 8.00am sharp, Giles came knocking at my home. I picked up my case, checked my tickets, passport and wallet, shook hands with the wife (we've never been a particularly emotional pair!), tried unsuccessfully to pretend that it really wouldn't be that exciting without her by my side, and like two schoolboys on their way to their first summer camp, our journey began. Then it stopped. Disaster! I had forgotten my sunglasses. California without shades – I could get arrested by the cool police. Giles stopped and I ran back. Two minutes later and now struggling to see through sunglasses and a foggy Yorkshire February morning we set off again.

God, I thought, I love this job! We had booked the cheapest possible tickets which meant flying Humberside to Amsterdam, and then Amsterdam to New York JFK, a short stay in the Big Apple allowing us to visit the American Museum of Natural History and then on to Detroit before finally on to San Francisco and a hire car to Monterey Bay. We could not have known that by the end of the journey we would understand the meaning of the term air rage.

It began to go wrong at Humberside. "Come on you two, we've got to go right now!" David was beckoning us from the airport entrance, he appeared flustered. He was dressed in tweed jacket and hat and was waving frantically for us to follow him. The check-in clerk quickly explained that there were high winds over Amsterdam and that our little 16-seater plane was having a panic attack and was threatening to refuse to take off. We would have to leave right now on an earlier, bigger and less timid plane. Outside not a piece of litter, not a leaf, not a cloud moved in the still morning air. Nevertheless, not to go would risk us missing our connection – to go would mean leaving Keith German all alone in a strange airport to sort out his own transport arrangements. We carefully weighed up the options for five seconds. "We'll go," we chorused.

Amsterdam airport was truly a global village; every nationality on earth seemed to be there apparently all united by the desire to be somewhere else and until that became possible, to buy consumer electricals. The concrete hinterland spread out from our terminal as far as bleary eyes could see. The threatened gale had now risen to its climax and was officially designated gentle breeze status!

At Amsterdam we met with John Czarky and his colleagues Andrew and Sor Lan Tan, his Chinese exhibition cost consultant. Soon we were out over the Atlantic. Almost eight cramped hot tiring hours later, KLM flight 160 began its descent into the New York evening. I had opted for the seat closest to the window whilst Giles had opted for one closest to the drinks trolley and so as we approached New York I could see nothing but lights. New York literally went from horizon to horizon. No landmarks at this height, just the overwhelming power of a city on steroids.

Once at JFK we made our way through customs, where a uniformed and square-jawed official checked my passport. "Been to the U.S. before?" he asked in an accent straight out of NYPD. "Just once to Orlando," I replied, trying hard not to sound like Dick Van Dyke. "Did yer see Mickey?" he asked. I smiled; I was unused to joking with anyone wearing a Colt 45. "What yer doing in New York?" "We're building a Natural History Museum of the Sea in Hull, England and we've come to see the New York Museum of Natural History and then on to Monterey Bay to see the aquarium."

"A museum, eh". For the first time he looked up. "You should be proud of that."

"I am" I said and for the first time I realised no one had ever given me or the team permission to be proud before. I suppose the closest had been the round of applause we received at the Christmas lights ceremony, but that had been more of a 'well done'. We had been given permission to feel scared, guilty, stupid, and both overly ambitious and lacking in ambition, but pride was something the English felt uncomfortable with confusing it with arrogance. Pride was something that only went before a fall.

Given the size of our party, it had been cheaper to hire a chauffeur-driven stretch limo than to use yellow cabs to get from the airport to the hotel, so David, with a speed that would have made an old politburo member blush, grabbed the best seat and sat back, fiddled with every button within reach – and several that were not, and eventually settled back and enjoyed the ride as though born to it.

The next day we rose to a cold New York's winter morning and walked through a deserted Central Park to the New York Museum of Natural History. We had already arranged for one of their curators to show us their new Earth Gallery and especially the black smoker display, the only one in the world. These strange intricate yet monolithic pillars seemed both ordinary and yet magical. We stared at the massive grey stones encrusted with the smallest evidence of life and realised that it was the fact that they were real which fascinated us. As we saw more of the exhibition we also noticed how they had resolved a question which we had considered ourselves on a number of occasions, namely, at what level, or age range to aim the text at. For each of their graphic panel displays they had a headline, no more than a dozen words in large clear type, which encapsulated the story. This was then expanded into a single paragraph in smaller type, taking the reader deeper into the subject before, finally, in small but still legible print, in which the story was expanded into some detail. This hierarchy of information seemed to fit our needs well and we were later to use it shamelessly.

We left the New York Museum of Natural History having learnt two important lessons: firstly, that The Deep would have to have some real objects on the dry side to add authenticity but also to release the sense of awe we were aiming for; and, secondly, that any text-based information would need to be layered.

That evening we stood in the hotel bar listening to a live Motown tribute band and tapping our feet in that almost rhythmical way which is the closest true Englishmen ever get to dancing. The conversation was all of exhibitions, of plans and brands and of course our coming trip to sunny California.

Outside in the already cold New York night, a furious cold front was heading towards us with the speed of a jet plane; unfortunately it was the only thing of any speed heading our way. By the next morning New York and its airports were snowbound.

In desperation, someone suggested driving to California then apologised as it was pointed out that this would take approximately two weeks. The earliest our plane would now be able to leave was tomorrow morning; we would arrive in California at 3.00 am and have to be up at 8.00 am for our rendezvous. Still, to go back to Hull and explain to our sponsors and to the Board that we never actually got to Monterey seemed unattractive. On the plus side, this was to be the opening day of the new Rose Gallery and we would now have a spare day to visit it.

Although it told the story of the Universe rather than the Oceans the Rose Gallery had many similarities with The Deep. Set in a massive glass box, visitors ascend a ramp, which wound around a scale model of the sun, which dominated the exhibit. Once inside the exhibition proper, the story of the Big Bang was used as an introduction, which in turn led onto a further ramped journey and timeline charting the development of the galaxy to the present day. At the end of the ramp, visitors broke out into a general exploratory space not unlike our proposals for Deep Blue One.

The exhibition, although excellent in its own way, was clearly not finished. Workmen were still fixing lights to fascias. Tape held together display panels and dangerously sharp edges were everywhere. The Press however, both in the U.S. and we later found, at home in the UK loved it. The English Press enthused about how the Rose Gallery expressed the confidence of the American people, in a way in which the Millennium Dome did not do for the British.

It is difficult, having been to both, not to feel that this comparison was unfair. If the Dome and the Rose Gallery were in each other's country, would not the press have praised the scale and global ambition of the Dome in establishing a new relationship between education and entertainment?

For us though, the main difference was not in scale, quality or funding but in the simple truth that the Rose Gallery had a clear story, it had a beginning, a middle and an end and it had a credibility in telling that story which the Dome, to be fair, never tried to achieve.

Again we learnt a number of lessons from the Rose Gallery but mostly we learnt that our vision for The Deep, as being scientifically robust but telling an interesting story from beginning to end, was right.

That evening Sor Lan offered to book an authentic Chinese restaurant for our evening meal in China Town and on arrival we were immediately refused entry until Sor Lan arrived in the following taxi. The restaurant was straight out of Tiananmen Square and even the most adventurous gourmets amongst us realised our limitations.

Giant dried shark fins decorated the walls, in our innocence they were remarked on only for their size and novelty. Only much later were we all to learn of the cruelty and environmental damage that shark finning causes.

The anti –finning campaign was to become a cause that The Deep would later put a lot of energy into supporting.

Our hastily amended travel plan was now to fly to Detroit and catch a connection to San Francisco. We would have an hour to relax in Detroit where we could, if not exactly see the sights of Motor City (if there are any), at least grab a coffee. Unfortunately we left New York exactly one hour late.

At Detroit we were informed that the San Francisco flight was now boarding at gate 26. Whilst I ran on ahead, Dave and some of our less nimble companions commandeered an electric baggage cart and its elderly lady driver sped them along the concourse. The cart twisted and turned as its portly baggage clung to it from every available purchase point. With Dave prominent in his tweed hat and jacket, the over-riding impression was of an episode of Miss Marple meets the Keystone Kops.

I arrived at gate 26 moments before the cart to learn that due to yet another change in plan, our flight was now leaving from gate 1 in 5 minutes, 2 of which were spent by Dave arguing with the desk clerk. After another brief episode of Wacky Races we boarded our flight with just seconds to spare.

We arrived in California in the dark and so when I awoke the next morning in my hotel room in Monterey Bay and drew back the curtains, the contrast to the chill and grey of New York was immediate. Outside cherry blossom trees frothed in what felt like spring sunshine. The early morning joggers, tanned and slim in their designer trainers ,glided past in the street beyond which the Pacific spread out across the horizon.

Monterey Bay itself was a town of picturesque white-panelled houses and small hotels tumbling down to a waterfront of rock and kelp, where sea otters dived and played in the surf. At the heart of the town was Cannery Row, and in what looked like an original sardine cannery, was Monterey Aquarium. We had heard of this place in one of our original conversations with Phil Crane, an aquarium in a city of 30,000 which had 1.7 million visitors in its first year. It was generally accepted as the standard by which other aquariums were judged, but which few if any ever matched. Monterey Bay was legendary amongst even the somewhat egotistical aquarium community.

It was Presidents' Weekend in the States and the aquarium was expecting a busy day. A member of the aquarium's staff met us at the gate and began to show us around. The displays were in two halves, the original part dominated by a kelp forest tank probably 4 metres by 7 metres round, using water taken directly from the Bay. This had led over the years to an intricate and colourful display as the many tiny sea creatures brought in from the ocean had developed a living eco-system of their own.

The graphic panels accompanying the tanks were, our guide modestly informed us, seldom read and contained too much detail for the general visitor. This however was of little concern as they ran a massive volunteer guide programme with over 80 trained individuals who 'simply enjoyed helping.'

As we explored further there was no denying the imagination and vision of those behind the original idea. Long before it was known that aquariums could be popular, these people - namely the Hewlett Packard family -had taken the public aquarium through its glass ceiling of imagination. In our own modest way, we hoped to do the same.

The second half of the displays formed part of the new extension. Here the displays were treated almost as works of art. Jellyfish, vivid orange ghosts were displayed against a simple electric blue background. Schooling fish swam constantly in one direction round an overhead dome of water. The art gallery feel was accentuated by the other surface treatments and it was an approach we had dismissed after our experiences in Portugal. Monterey Bay however had begun to successfully integrate what we called wet and dry exhibits into a more holistic visitor experience. Specifically they had floating acrylic magnifying glasses in the touch pool, allowing visitors to view under the surface. They also had simple brass rubbing plates in an area set aside for the under 7s. Once again we were to use these and other Monterey ideas in The Deep.

They also however had 'MBARI', the Monterey Bay Research Institute, funded from a multimillion-dollar endowment from Hewlett Packard which carried out detailed scientific research into the complex and diverse Monterey Bay area, feeding the aquarium with new information and stories to refresh the exhibits. This was an area we were still lacking in. Despite the University research areas in The Deep, we could not yet feed directly from any such source.

We were finally shown into a private area which appeared to be reserved for special guests and corporate hospitality. As if to emphasise its status as one of the world's great aquariums this room had an entire viewing window of acrylic almost 15 metres in length, into their display on the El-Niño effect. A window more than twice as big as anything planned at The Deep, and not even on public display. We felt if not defeated, at least deflated as, over a coffee, I began to explain our own objectives and displays with our host.

We were pleased and somewhat surprised at his response to our plans; rather than politely dismissing them he seemed genuinely impressed and became quite animated when shown building elevations and exhibition layouts. We left with perhaps our first indication that whilst what we had planned would not compare or compete with Monterey Bay it may, nonetheless, be of international significance. If we could raise an eyebrow or two in this, the Mecca of aquariums...who knows?

That evening eager to make the most of any free time we had left in the Sunshine State, Giles, Keith and I agreed to meet up and explore further. The options were impressive; the Pacific Ocean around Monterey Bay was home to migrating Grey Whales, whilst sea otters were common along the whole of the rocky coast. The town itself still echoed with John Steinbeck's characters and their haunts. To the south lay the City of Angels and Hollywood, whilst to the North, San Francisco. After careful consideration we made our way to Monterey Bay's only English pub.

In reality of course, the Americans could only achieve an approximation of our Great English Institution. They had not properly considered the myriad of subtle cultural influences which interplay to create such a successful formula. The beer for example was served cold, in clean glasses. The barmaid was friendly, whilst the total lack of either an Irish theme or Japanese Karaoke failed to place it in either of the two authentic sub species, which now make up the genre.

The pub was populated by a dozen or so locals who had clearly been excluded from all the better bars around and whose last gainful employment appeared to have been as extras in the film Deliverance. They stopped talking when we entered and in a scene equally reminiscent of a Western movie or indeed a Welsh-speaking pub, viewed us in a vaguely threatening way. As Giles went for some drinks, Keith suggested a game of darts partly to break the silence, partly I suspected in order to become armed. Rather than lowering our profile however, this only served to focus the whole pub's attention on these two Englishmen playing their national sport, badly!

Eventually I ground down the innate hostility of the dartboard to arrive at double one. I stepped up to the oche for what I felt sure would be the first of many such visits and took aim. "Betcha a dollar he kent git it wid three darts!" the challenge came loud and clear from the rear of the pub. Those present whose attention had drifted during the long and uneventful match shifted in their chairs and refocused. My first dart missed by an inch, my second by slightly less.

"Hi what's up dudes?" The Lucky Little Devil finally arrived like the English version of the 7th cavalry. He wore a baseball cap back to front and a Lakers' basketball kit complete with Nike trainers. "You could have told me you were going up the pub," he said. He pulled up a bar stool and ordered Devil's Advokaat.

My third dart hit dead centre of double one. "You owe me a dollar," I said as smugly as I could manage. In Heaven, Mad King George punched the air in celebration. Keith wisely suggested we leave and join the others before any other type of punching could begin.

At dinner that evening, Giles and I joined John Czarky and Andrew Wood Walker at their table and we reviewed some of the lessons we had learnt. Firstly, we felt that the Big Bang exhibition we had seen in New York was equally relevant to our story; although not exactly original in an exhibition sense, it could provide us with the dramatic beginning we still sought, our first "wow factor". This would, however, raise three other questions. Firstly, whilst the big bang was relevant as the origin of all time, space and the elements that would one day go on to form the oceans, it did not fulfil the role of an introduction, which would need to be more specifically ocean based and would need to introduce some of the themes which the rest of the exhibitions explored, such as the interconnectedness of land and sea. A map of the world showing the major ocean masses was proposed along with a short introductory film, but a conventional map only ever shows the land in any detail, relegating the oceans to a flat blue desert. Over coffee, it was observed that the global warming interactive which we had tentatively pencilled in for this area was trying to tell two separate stories. Firstly it showed the topography of the undersea world and yet also tried to explain the issues of global sea level change. By separating these themes we could use a 3D topographical map of the sea bed as part of our introduction and place the global sea level interactive more appropriately within the admittedly weak Polar gallery. We had seen such a 3D map of the undersea landscape modelled in white card in Portugal and had been impressed by the alternative view of the sea that it gave. White card wouldn't stand up to a busy exhibition so ours would need to be both more robust and more tactile. It felt right though, to greet customers with an image which challenged the conventional view of the sea, and which provided an introduction showing not the world with its oceans but what the world would look like without them.

Secondly, the Big Bang sequence seemed to underline even further that we could not mix scientifically robust messages with stories of myth and legend. Words and Ideas had years previously suggested that sea monsters and myths would be a commercially sound theme, but their inclusion was becoming more and more problematic.

Were we a science centre or a theme park? If myths were to be included anywhere it seemed increasingly clear that they would have to be dealt with as an explanation of the way mankind has viewed the oceans before the age of science; thus myths and legends became the modest, pre-show.

Later we were to link the myth and the science by theming the first fish tank to become a stranger than fiction tank, raising the question whether legend is in fact any stranger than the reality of fish that can walk, or of fish that look every inch like a lemon that's swallowed a box!

We also used the junction between the story of myth and the world of science to introduce a much bigger question, which now straddles the exhibition's entry "In the beginning God created the heavens and the earth and the earth was without form and void and darkness was upon the face of The Deep." The fact that visitors would enter under this quotation into darkness, to witness the moment of creation was deliberate, even if the reference to The Deep was a bit fortuitous. More fundamentally the inclusion of this quotation at the junction between the myths and the science is intended to raise in visitors' minds the biggest question of all.

From now on it would be a golden rule that everything past this point in the exhibition would be scientifically robust.

On returning home, we wrote to all other major religious groups in Hull to ask if their Holy book had similar quotations but never received any replies.

The introduction area of the displays had now taken on its final form, the downside was that the establishment of the Big Bang theatre would further erode the space available on the third floor for catering, but the architect had yet to fully define this area and so the exhibition had first call.

I arrived home still buzzing from all we had seen and planned over the last few days. My head was full of a thousand tasks that we still had to do. Tomorrow I would have to check on Ossie's progress on a ground-breaking ceremony, and talk to Neil about a couple of planning problems. We had a meeting at 9am and I had a presentation to the University at 7pm.

The house was empty and dark and Nicky's car and both our girls were gone. Nicky had left a hastily written message on the table, which simply read, Ring Mum. Lisa, our youngest daughter, had been rushed into hospital with a serious breathing problem. I later found out that at one point Nicky thought we might lose her.

It reminded me that this had not only been my journey, but that my family had been through it with me, it reminded me that they were paying a price every bit as high as I was. My absences, the long hours, the stress and my mood swings were theirs to endure as much as they were mine.

CHAPTER 21 SPRING 2000

ON YOUR MARKS... GET SET....WAIT

"Aristotle maintained that women had fewer teeth than men. Although he was married twice it never occurred to him to verify this statement by looking in his wives' mouth."

Bertrand Russell

The displays continued to evolve. Giles, Dave and I had developed more of a game than an intellectual process which involved focusing on the weakest part of the displays and asking how it could be improved. It was a devil-take-the-hindmost editing process. An example of this process was that of The Deep Theatre, the last of the large exhibition spaces.

After a day of mind-numbing meetings and bickering consultants, Giles and I needed to reconnect with the fun bits of the project and so we sat sipping the remains of some red wine left over from Christmas. It was that part of the day when our conscientiousness was too great to allow us to go home, but not great enough to motivate us to carry out any constructive work. Giles began our favourite parlour game: "So what's the worst part of the exhibition?" We retraced the route again in our imaginations. Myths and Legends....Big Bang....ramped walkway and fossil wall... lagoon ...coral wall... main tank...the poles and then at ground floor level The Deep Theatre before an exit which included the world's first underwater lift ride to the surface.

It was the so-called Deep Theatre, it just didn't work; the story was a journey through time and depth.... except for the end which was a film show! The Chairman's mantra that we must have a story applied to two thirds of The Deep but was being conveniently forgotten about at its climax. The plan as it currently existed was for some form of as yet unspecified audiovisual theatre showing a film presentation. This gave us two problems: firstly, we had decided months ago not to go for a large format film theatre and the space simply did not exist anymore to do it successfully; and, secondly, we had also opted for a linear route not a pulsed exhibition. A "show" at which people would have to gather and be seated in a group conflicted with this.

We would have a steady stream of visitors flowing into a space where they would be gathered before being released en masse into the final lift rides which would be unable to cope.

The film presentation was important however as it would give us the ability to install new films from time to time giving us something that was difficult to achieve in aquariums, namely a changing exhibit, but it just didn't fit. By now we had really begun to see three parallel stories emerging: that of a journey through depth from outer space onto the surface of the Ocean, and through a shallow coral lagoon down into the deep ocean; a second journey through time from the formation of the seas, through the present day and forward into a possible future; and finally a journey, if not along the Meridian line, then at least from Equator to pole. However, all three of these stories' had to come together at the end, and they didn't. The answer we came up with wasn't difficult; it was spotting that we were ignoring the question which had been the problem.

We agreed that rather than a Deep Theatre, we would instead theme the area as a futuristic Deep sea research station. It would have "live" film feeds coming from around the globe and would set itself missions ranging from a census of whales and dolphins to threats to the polar ice caps. It would be set on the Deep ocean floor and complete our journey through time and through depth. Geographically we could position it anywhere on earth we wished so even the pole-to-pole storyline wouldn't jar. The live stream style of film we had in mind would be more like a 24hour news channel than a documentary film and would therefore allow us to avoid the need to pulse visitors, allowing them to view as much or as little as they wished.

Ironically it was a return to one of the very first concepts we had been given by Words and Ideas. Their concept for the whole exhibition had been of a futuristic deep sea research station, but it had been completely lost once the designs for the original building were discarded; now it returned and resolved one of the last real dilemmas we had on the exhibitions.

Another example of this process came during a conversation with David Gemmell. David noted that the final circumnavigation of the main tank had become a bit of an anti-climax. The water pressure made it difficult to place anything bigger than a small window at this depth without it becoming too thick and expensive. Thus all the best views of the main tank were early on in the display. The problem, Dave claimed, was that The Deep had lost its underwater tunnel. We had criticised other aquariums for having long, somewhat tedious tunnels that seemed to go on forever. We had nonetheless wanted a tunnel of some sort, but through one of the many stages of the design and budget trimming process it had, we now realised, disappeared.

David's response was simply to insist that the architect put back our tunnel. Of course there was opposition from some members of the design team but Dave has a way of simply and calmly getting his way, as I knew better than most! The result is there today, probably the world's deepest viewing tunnel and undoubtedly one of the stars of The Deep. Together Dave's tunnel and the switching of the concept of The Deep Theatre to what would soon become known as "Deep Blue One" clarified and transformed the story.

It was possible to spot this cosy group amnesia relatively frequently during the project; it was a sort of a sub-species of the famous "Group Think" phenomenon portrayed so powerfully as President Kennedy grappled with the Bay of Pigs proposal. In brief, the theory goes that if you surround yourself with likeminded individuals who believe the same things and want to be part of the team, no one will question the perceived wisdom of the Group.

Whilst that does exist in our English culture, we suffer more from a related syndrome, something which might best be described as "Groups don't think". In Groups don't Think, all members of a group are perfectly well aware of the problem but no one ever mentions it either because the unspoken consensus is that it is too difficult to resolve, or that in airing a problem for which you (and you suspect everyone else) has no answer you will just be seen as difficult and negative. Worse still, if you raise the question to which there is no answer you might be the poor sod who is tasked with resolving it!

For Giles and me, alone, and with our inhibitions suitably eroded by the Merlot we were able to say what we had both been thinking for a while: that The Deep Theatre was a crappy idea! Once articulated, the solution had come quickly.

If we were to keep to schedule we had to start clearing the site and constructing the flood defences and so Ossie pushed ahead with the ground-breaking ceremony. Ossie and his team, particularly Linda, organised the morning with Charlie Dimmock in the starring role. Charlie was wonderful, particularly with the local children who performed for the assembled crowd of dignitaries. Ossie asked me to host the VIP event, whilst he handled the press and TV. At last we were up and running. A few days later the site began to be cleared in preparation for the letting of the main building contract. The soil was, as expected, pretty contaminated and was so full of heavy metals that it was touch and go as to whether or not we removed it or mined it. The pollution had come from an old ship repair yard which, until relatively recently, had occupied our site. It had been called Cook, Welton and Gemmells, and, we later discovered, had once been owned by David's great great great uncle. The fact that the Chairman's ancestors had built here before was intriguing.

With Ossie fully occupied with the construction process I was finding it difficult to step back from those aspects of project which needed more of an operational focus, and I soon began to worry again about our lack of progress on the issues surrounding the stocking and running of an aquarium. Whilst lots of us felt qualified to dabble in the dry side exhibits, the marine biology was far more difficult. To date we had between us not even been able to come up with a sensible species list and as such our brief to the architect and to IAT to design tanks for "some sharks, rays and shoaling fish" was becoming problematic. This role was really down to Ian Cunningham from Real Life Leisure, but for some reason the list was proving difficult to obtain.

Ossie meanwhile seemed to have taken something of a dislike to Ian and this deteriorating relationship seemed to promise to delay a species list further. Eventually after much encouragement Real Life Leisure duly delivered a species list. It obviously included several species of rays, shoaling fish, moray eels and of course sharks. The largest of the shark species being recommended were Sand Tiger sharks which would grow to about 4 metres but which arrive at about 2m in length.

Sand Tigers, or Ragged Tooths as the Australians call them, are seen in a lot of the bigger aquariums, but they do require rather careful handling. They are unlikely, for example, to agree to climb six flights of stairs and get themselves into the main tank. This seemed to surprise the design team which had failed to consider how we would get large sharks in and out of the main tank. Again I could sense another of those "Groups don't Think" issues. We had all realised, of course, that at some point we would have to get a number of large sharks into the tank, but nobody had wanted to look like the stupid one and ask how this was to be achieved. How does one receive delivery of a shark? How do you keep it alive on a journey from the tropics to Hull, and then when it does arrive how do you get a 2m shark up three storeys and into an aquarium without a) removing it from water which we felt was probably a bad thing, or b) inadvertently supplementing its diet with one or more staff members? The answer was somehow both obvious and implausible: a shark coffin. The sharks would be sedated to reduce stress (on the shark not the handlers) and placed in what was basically a small self-contained aquarium; the coffin would then be placed in one of our lifts and taken to the quarantine area on the third floor.

We quickly wrote to those responsible for specifying the lifts and informed them of our requirements, and were relieved when we found out that we had just been in time to make the changes. At least for now, that problem could be solved. Where you actually buy a 2m shark from, however, we as yet had no idea! The whole episode had again illustrated two things: firstly, that whilst we had no intention of operating The Deep we knew very little about running an aquarium and that lack of knowledge risked us making big design mistakes ; and, secondly, it showed how even a small delay in a seemingly trivial piece of work could have massive consequences. The good news was that we were at last beginning to understand how much we didn't know, but that hardly seemed to provide much reassurance in the circumstances.

The first few construction-related contracts for things like flood defences and ground clearance were now ready to be let, and all came in either on budget or slightly below. Given the generous level of contingencies we had built in, and despite the £1.7m funding gap proving stubbornly difficult to reduce, all appeared to be going well, but appearances can of course be deceptive!

The design of the building itself was complex but the programme called for immediate decisions and left little time for problem solving. For example even at this late stage, the architect had been unable to resolve the issues surrounding the cafe. The fundamental problem was that the space available for catering, shop, offices and storage had all been drastically reduced over the years. Now it would have needed the machine from "Honey I shrunk the kids" (either the original or the sequel) to get our expected visitor numbers into the catering space we had. The Board had been adamant that the café should retain the dramatic river views but the space available had been eroded firstly by the budget crisis and then by the inclusion of the retail area within the same space and finally by our decision taken in California to put the Big Bang Theatre in part of the space designated for catering.

It was now totally unworkable.

Ossie and the design team considered the options at yet another away day. Lines were drawn and redrawn but the problem remained. Finally, the architect's representative proposed something which might have sounded logical from a design perspective but which was unthinkable from a commercial point of view. Namely that we lose the retail area entirely, returning the whole of the remaining space to catering.

The Deep would simply have no shop. Ian Cunningham, who until then had said little, reacted in the way one might have expected. This sort of non-commercial decision was exactly what he as a future operator had feared from the earliest talk of icon buildings. He was already unhappy with the lack of priority given to the shop and about the fact that it was on the first floor, and so this was the final straw.

He threw his arms up in exasperation. "For all it matters you might as well do away with the shop, it's in completely the wrong position anyway, everyone can see it should be there, where people enter and leave the building not stuck up there where no one will use it." He poked an ill-tempered finger at that part of the plan which showed the entrance. "The whole bloody entrance area doesn't work anyway." He was right. Again "Groups don't Think" had us all in a position where we knew that the entrance, as it was currently conceived, which led straight into a lift would be a nightmare to manage and a complete turn-off for visitors, but without an alternative and with so many other problems awaiting our attention we had established an unspoken agreement not to raise the issue.

Whereas it had taken alcohol for Giles and me to articulate the problem with The Deep Theatre, it had taken a fit of temper for Ian to do the same with the shop and entrance areas. Next day, Ossie briefed me on the debate and asked for my support in asking the Board to agree a low-cost extension to the building. The extension could provide a proper reception area, a ground floor retail space which was not only on the main visitor route but could also be accessed by the non-exhibition visitor. From an operational point of view we could also cover ticket and retail sales with a single member of staff during off-peak times. Architecturally too the low-cost extension worked as it continued the line of the building on its eastern elevation counteracting the stumpy profile it had taken on since the last big budget crisis. I needed no convincing, and to be fair neither did the Board.

Thanks to Ian and Ossie we had avoided a Pooh trap big enough to hold not only a bear of very little brain but Tigger, Roo and half of Christopher Robin's classmates.

Taking these late changes in his stride, Terry Farrell and his team quickly redrew the plans yet again.

For weeks little appeared to be happening on site. Slowly the site was being cleared, flood defences installed and foundations and piling were begun but too often there seemed to be long gaps when progress seemed to slow or stop entirely. Our monthly project team meetings were long and tedious as each consultant rehashed reasons for delays in their own areas whilst criticising delays from others. The architects continued to develop the detailed designs , which given the complexities of the building meant extra work by the structural engineers, mechanical and electrical consultants and crucially water treatment specialists. Conscious of the need to push on we were determined to help the process by keeping any client changes to a minimum. It gradually became clear though that in many cases changes were not being initiated by us and yet we were being given little choice but to agree to changes proposed by the design team itself, as not do so would have been irresponsible. For example, we were once asked if we would agree to a change after it had been discovered that one of the lift shafts appeared to take a small dog leg turn to the right between the second and third floors. At this stage of course it wasn't expensive to resolve the problem but nevertheless it was logged as a client change. Another example was that by now the University had replaced Jack Hardisty's Humber Observatory with a flume tank capable of modelling real estuarine environments and Professor Kopp from our Board had been asked by the University to head up this aspect of the project. In our inaugural meeting on the subject Ekkehard and I discovered that, firstly someone had moved a wall surrounding the University Flume Tank and that the Flume could no longer fit into the space provided; secondly that if it could be made to fit then the electricity supply was insufficient to run the massive pumps that it required; and that thirdly the Health and Safety advisers would not allow the Flume to be used with the current level of access. All three problems, however, were likely to be academic as the piling which by now was already in place had not been designed for the weight of the sand and gravel which the flume tank would need to carry. One by one we resolved these problems but the idea of client discipline in resisting changes was a joke.

Perhaps most damaging were the times when we were asked for an immediate decision so as not to delay the build, only to find that the consequences of the change had not been thought through properly by the team. Probably the biggest of these was my decision to move the water treatment system from the empty slipway adjacent to the main building into the building itself. We had been advised by the design team that it would save £100,000. What we were not, however, told is that it would also affect the steel structure of the building and be used by said team as a further reason for significant delay and redesign.

With so much of the design still fluid it seemed particularly unfair when we were told that one of the few issues which we as a client wanted to mull over for a while longer, namely the exact size and position of the major viewing windows into the main tank needed to be made at once. The reality was however that this was an absolutely fundamental decision. The main windows into the open ocean tank are 7m by 3m and weigh the same as an Asian elephant. They are amongst the biggest single pieces of acrylic in the world, so clearly the builders needed to think about how to get then into the building. When we realised that there were only two manufacturers of such windows in the world, one in the U.S. and the other in Japan and that both have waiting lists and delivery times which together would take many months, then we began to understand that the need for speed was genuine. With the help of the architect and a simple model of the main tank we spent a surreal day peering like Gulliver into this tiny cardboard aquarium, sticking card over unwanted views cutting away at the model until we were satisfied that we had it right. The secret was to get as many views into the main tank as possible without being able to see other people staring back at you, but in such a deep tank (10 metres) we would also have to bear in mind that the acrylic would need to get thicker and therefore more expensive as the water gets deeper. So the biggest windows would have to be higher up in the journey. We soon reached a position where we felt confident enough to order the panels, and not a moment too soon. If any of them were to arrive damaged or were broken or scratched during transport or installation we would not be open in time.

As the letting of major contracts began in earnest it was clear that contractor's prices were creeping up and were now beginning to reflect not only the uncertainty of the current design but also an emerging building boom generally.

The steel-contract was a good example. Firstly, the structural engineers discovered that an additional 30% more steelwork would be required than originally expected (see above decision on the water treatment system), whilst the detailed designs of the interfaces between the various steel members proved so complex that the contractors computer programs could not cope, requiring each junction to be calculated by hand using essentially the same technology as Khufu used to build his Pyramid.

The eventual price of the steel was well over £100,000 more than our budget. Whilst all this was worrying, we continued to be reassured that our level of contingencies was adequate and that the unexpected was after all, exactly what they were there to cover. Whenever we asked about the programme we were told that any delay could be made up later.

In parallel with the construction process we were trying to push on with consideration of who and how the eventual operational phase would be handled when Ian Cunningham from Real Life Leisure, who had been our operations consultant since Phil Crane's departure, unexpectedly sold his company to Grant Leisure who in effect inherited Ian's role on our team. Grant Leisure were very professional and helpful; they showed none of the resistance which both Phil and Ian had shown at various times. They were, however, never really accepted by the wider team. Firstly being operational they were seen by some as irrelevant to the day-to-day, minute-by-minute problems of the construction process, but most importantly they had come to the table late and by a route few thought legitimate. Like a son or daughter who gets their seat on the Board by an inheritance, Grant Leisure had much to prove and little time to do it. My Board were also uncomfortable. They had, they felt, appointed Ian personally and they now found themselves with little choice but to agree to the transfer of the contract.

The funding gap, which had quietly crept up to over £2m, now began to creep up further with every day that passed, and for the first time I really began to understand the position we (and any client using the form of contract we had chosen) were in. In short, we had been under the impression that our Quantity Surveyors had a reasonable grasp on the probable costs of the project. They were, however, working with incomplete designs to an unachievable construction programme and had, it now transpired, simply taken the original budget as it had previously existed and attempted to apportion that across the new emerging design. I'm no expert, but this seemed like checking your wallet and seeing you had £5.00 to spend on lunch then eating at Gordon Ramsay's and explaining to him that you had only allocated £3.00 for your main course and the rest for a pudding.

Whilst technically my role on the project was now only that of the Council's observer, Ossie was happy that Keith was keeping me fully informed - but I wasn't! Indeed

I began to dread the regular phone calls from Keith German the project manager. "The brickwork and block work package has come back with a price from the contractors, are you sitting down?" "We've struck a major problem with the cladding". " There's a problem with contamination on site," etc., etc. and as if our consultants weren't giving us enough to worry about, it was now that Giles helpfully decided to check whether the sound from the fog horn situated just yards from the point of the building would affect the fish in our exhibitions.

That weekend, at the end of March 2000, as I lay on my back next to my garden pond, the whole project seemed capable of redefining the phrase "White Elephant". We were on a white water raft, swept by events from one foaming rapid to the next. We weren't steering the project. We were simply trying to push it away from the more deadly looking rock faces. By now at least I was no longer carrying the project alone; the organisation had grown into what felt like a very different one, from its original partners. Although still small, only about 6 or 7 people, it was clearly focused on its task. Dr Giles Davidson, now the Company secretary, had organised a new office suite away from the Council which seemed to go a long way from separating The Deep's crew from the Council in terms of culture and working practices. Neil Porteus, one of the group accountants in the Council, had been seconded full time to the project, primarily to carry on with the mountain of work associated with all these funding bodies but also to keep an eye on the project in general from the Council's point of view which after all remained the ultimate guarantor. With Giles and Neil were Louise Kirby who became Ossie's secretary, Diane Porter and Linda Martin from the Tourism Section of my Department. Linda Martin who had joined some months earlier was dealing with PR, an increasing important role and one that Ossie himself was particularly keen to become involved in.

For all of its problems on the construction front The Deep now had an independent Board, a Chief Executive, Company Secretary, Finance Director and Public Relations machine in place. We had good reason to believe that the final pieces of the funding package were either in place or on the way and the steel skeleton of the building had begun to take shape against the sky line. It was against this background that I was asked to go and see the Chief Executive of the Council, Ian Crookham.

I waited for a few moments in Ian's anteroom before he came out and asked me into his panelled office. One wall was covered by a dark oak bookcase containing Council minutes back to before the war. Whilst these gave an impression of a

Chief Executive imbued in the intricacies of Council minutes I knew that this was not the case. I wondered briefly what books Ian kept hidden in his top drawer and suspected that they might have titles like *Dealing with Difficult People*, *Thriving on Chaos* by Tom Peters and *The Age of Unreason* by Charles Handy.

Ian and I had been Chief Officers together and I would like to think had always had a mutual respect for each other, I can remember that at a social event once his wife confided to mine that Ian likes to play computer games where he pilots a complex aircraft into a safe landing; my wife had replied that I too play computer games but mostly those where I play the role of god!! I always thought that this probably said something about both of our personalities!

Ian began: "I have been thinking that given the position that The Deep now finds itself in, this might be a good time for you to take a step back." He went on quickly as if to avoid any interruption: "I am quite happy if you carry on taking a role in the exhibitions, but with Mr Hall in place and the Board now working well I think it is probably best, certainly from the Council's point of view, if we let it go its own way. We always knew that the Council wouldn't want to be seen running a visitor attraction quite like The Deep, you must surely have been expected this?" I explained to Ian that this really was no big deal for me; I felt my role had come to a natural conclusion and having given birth to The Deep I could perfectly well see that it should now be left to learn to fly on its own. Ian seemed surprised, either by my mixed metaphor or that I was so sanguine about letting my baby go, but as he quite rightly said it was no great surprise, this was to some extent what I had been looking forward to almost since the train journey back from the Natural History Museum: that I would one day be able to pass the project over to others but to do so from a position of strength not as a result of a disaster. Recently, my lovely bouncing baby was starting to look suspiciously like a monster anyway and, truth be told, I even felt a bit relieved We finished our coffee and indulged in a few minutes of officer politics before I left and returned to my department.

CHAPTER 22   SUMMER 2000

I AM SECONDED

"More people out of work leads to unemployment."
Calvin Coolidge

I liked being a Chief Officer; I liked being important enough to play officer politics rather than just bitching, although on the face of it they are quite similar, the main difference being in the level of complexity and subtlety needed. If bitching is like draughts, officer politics is like chess. There were in any event other reasons for wanting to return to the department. The Council was about to go through another officer restructuring, the Chief Officers in Hull have a similar life expectancy to a cheese burger at an Elvis convention, and there was going to be a lot of chess played in the next three months and I needed to be concentrating on my game.

I had once been told that if you are ever in any doubt as to how vital you are to an organisation you should place your hand in a bucket of water and the hole left when you remove it, is how much you will be missed. Whilst this says much about the motivational style of Local Government, I have to admit there is some truth in it. Large organisations do seem to be particularly adept at closing ranks to fill any managerial vacancy. It's normally only the managers themselves that think they are indispensable.

It should not have been the surprise that it was then when a few weeks later I attended a special meeting of the Council's Corporate Management team at which the new structure was revealed.

We sat politely as Ian Crookham and a particularly obese consultant struggled with an uncooperative flip chart until eventually Ian called the meeting to order and explained what everyone already knew was the reason for the meeting. We were to be re-organised to encourage more cross-departmental co-operation, the current management team of 10 was too large. I disagreed; the only thing that was too large in my opinion was the consultant who had by now collapsed into an easy chair seemingly exhausted by his endeavours with the flip chart.

Of course I said nothing, whatever the new structure; the appointment process for the jobs it contained began now. From now on management team would divide into two groups, those who were against the change, but who would support it in public in order to maximise their chances of survival, and those over 50 who were also against it, but would also support it in public least their chance of an early retirement and a Golden Handshake escape them.

As the new structure was revealed I scanned the pages for "my job". Whilst apprehensive, my department which represented only 5% of council staff had just received 50% of all the awards in the Council equivalent of the Oscars, and with The Deep site now being cleared to allow construction to begin and the Business Centre now well under way, I felt I had reason to be confident. Needless to say, this turned out to be far from the case. Leisure being the smallest Department had been divided up between the other big players, Education, Economic Development and Social Services.

Running an efficient high-profile Department had been a fundamental schoolboy error and with so much experience I should have known better. Every powerful councillor wanted the kudos from the museums, the publicity from Sports Events, and the votes from the Community Centres and of course the free tickets from the Theatres. Whereas who wanted to be called into the News at Ten studio whenever there was a Child Protection problem, or constantly harangued for the quality of the housing stock? Who wants to be Chair of the Education Committee in the worst performing education authority in England? My Leisure Department had been a veritable fruit bowl of fun, and in true socialist style it had been shared out equally. However, all was not lost; it would after all also mean that I had a legitimate claim on at least three jobs even if I would be the outsider in all of them.

When the interviews came along I felt my chances had increased considerably when I realised that the Councillor panel was asking exactly the same questions for each of the jobs. By my third and final interview I was word perfect, I left the interview with renewed confidence. My colleague and competitor for one of the posts met me on the way out. "How did it go?" "OK. To be honest it was probably the best interview I've ever had". "Well done" he replied, he seemed genuinely pleased for me. "You know you don't need to worry. You're well thought of, they'll find a role for you". "I took the Chairman of the panel to dinner yesterday, and he said as much".

Bugger! I thought I was good at this, but I wasn't in this guy's league. Not only was he a better manager than me (which I could accept), he was also a better creep.

Needless to say, he got the job and I was made Deputy Group Director of nothing in particular.

By the summer of 2000 the building was finally beginning to rise from its foundations. As yet the steel frame looked no more spectacular than a small forest of metal. The Business Centre, however, a much simpler building, had shot up quickly and was by now almost finished.

As the re-organisation at the Council worked its toxic way through the structure, it soon became clear that my new role as Deputy Group Director was about as useful as a chocolate sundial; clearly this was a job manufactured for me but which had no real role. Of course having nothing to do has its attractions, but in reality these soon fade, and you are left looking over your shoulder wondering how long it will be before the next restructuring, the one you won't survive. Whilst I was still involved in some minor aspects of The Deep such as planning the exhibitions etc., Ossie had by now established himself as the new boss and was taking more and more of a lead. Whatever my concerns over my personal circumstances at least I began to feel that The Deep was at last becoming an independent child. Its long-term success would be my best guarantee of staying in a job with the Council, or at least getting another one somewhere else.

It came as a particular shock then when Ossie, who had, it should be said, always had a range of other business interests, suddenly left in order to pursue them.

Immediately the press smelt a problem. One boss returns to the Council and is followed weeks later by another? What secret did we know that they didn't? Was The Deep about to turn bad? David asked me to return for a few days to steady the ship and deal with the press. It was to be a few days that would last the rest of my working life!

With Ossie's unexpected departure a wave of insecurity swept through Giles and his team. Ever since our first discussions with Phil Crane it had always been the intention that we would employ a private aquarium operator to run The Deep once it was opened but, of course, this meant that as the project moved closer to completion that everyone who worked for The Deep would become less and less secure, and this realisation suddenly seemed to be taking root in the team. David Gemmell moved quickly to ask if I would be prepared to be seconded from the Council to The Deep on a longer term basis, to provide some continuity and stability until a new Chief Executive could be appointed. I agreed and once more found myself in charge of the project.

The principle of secondment as a career development opportunity is ideal from the organisation's point of view. It is however almost never a good career move for the secondee. Once out of your office, the organisation tends to adapt to one's absence in less time than it takes to screw a new name plate to the office door. Whilst I was aware of this, the reality was that by now I had little to lose. For Neil Porteus however the equation was different. The project's accountant and already a Council secondee, Neil was concerned not to have the waters close over his career at the Council or to be left in increasing limbo as The Deep moved ever closer to its operation phase. Before I could take up the reins from Ossie, Neil resigned as our accountant and returned to the Council to take his chances there. Apart from the fact that Neil is an extremely talented finance officer, I had other reasons not to want to lose him. The press was already reading far too much into Ossie's resignation and against the failure of the Millennium Dome, losing a Chief Executive and a Finance Officer in a week might have become a public relations disaster from which it could have taken years to recover. So I went to see if I could convince Neil to come back. Neil had been involved in the project almost since its conception and like all of us had fallen in love with the idea of seeing it through. In truth, he took little convincing to rejoin the team but it was a brave decision on his part. The effort I made to convince him to return proved to be a defining moment in the life of The Deep.

Given the ever shortening timeframe Neil agreed with Giles and me that it would be a fruitless task to try and appoint a replacement for Ossie. Better to concentrate on finding an operational partner who could begin to prepare for the operational stage and who would be able to re-inject some commercial expertise into the final detailed design phase.

My second task then after seeing Neil was to draw up a draft contract to be advertised. There are two ways in which you can write a contract like this. The first, and the way I was accustomed to in Local Government, was to do so in order to defend an in-house contractor. Here you specify everything from the colour of the staff uniform to the size of the rubber on the supervisor's pencil. Such contracts had always seemed legitimate of course; the Council buying the service had probably had a policy on the acceptable colour for staff uniforms for some years. No reds, blues, yellows or greens as these were all associated with political parties, no blacks or brown shirts as these are still associated with Fascists or indeed whites as this could be associated with the Klu Klux Klan (ironically also Fascists) and certainly no horizontal stripes as the unions had objected to these because they made their members look fat. Whilst badly worn pencil erasers had been shown to expose dangerously sharp metal end pieces which could introduce a host of deadly pathogens into the bloodstream when the pencil was sucked. Not surprisingly, these type of contracts extend into several volumes and concentrate not on what needs to be achieved, but the way in which it is to be carried out.

The second way of approaching a contract was certainly more risky, and assumed the potential contractors were neither complete morons nor that their major purpose in life was to win a contract and then transform it into some Faustian pact with the Devil. Here you simply specify what you needed to be achieved and let the contractor get on with it.

I locked myself away in our small meeting room with a brand new writing pad, checked the rubber on the end of my pencil for sharp edges, (old habits die hard) and began to write the specification for our managing operator. Page 1, paragraph 1. Uniforms................Some weeks or so later I had at least a first draft ready, and sent the tome to Keith German for his comments. Unfortunately Keith failed to understand that when I - and indeed most bosses - ask subordinates for comments on their work they seldom either expect or require a response. What they are in fact seeking is to let their team know that they too are doing their bit and that their bit is indeed excellent.

I was somewhat taken aback then when Keith replied dismissing my entire document as overly long and bureaucratic. I tried again. What did we really want from an operator? We wanted The Deep opened, we wanted it run efficiently certainly but just as importantly we wanted a certain style, we wanted the same balance in an operator as had been shown in the design of the building. A balance between education and entertainment, between commercial success and our other agendas, quality, image, research etc. We also wanted a commercial operator to be a real partner, to share the risks and the rewards.

When this second contract was ready it was by far a more realistic and friendly document (by which I mean shorter) than my first attempt. We advertised the contract across Europe ,firstly in order to comply with the regulations of our European funders but also because Europe tends to have more of the charity-based aquariums that we felt might be a better match for us than the British operators, who despite their carefully crafted image are in reality almost entirely profit-driven. Sea Life centres had already indicated that, being by far the biggest kid on the block, they would not enter a bidding process. If we chose to ask them, they may be interested but only on the basis of a management contract; they would not share any of the risk. Whilst some of us had initially favoured working with Sea Life, their demands made it impossible for us to do so and remain inside the rules of our funders.

One by one the already short list of potential operators got shorter still, a process which culminated in a series of particularly gruelling interviews between the Board and the remaining hotchpotch of potential operators. At the end of the interviews it was clear that we would not be able to appoint, and so once again the idiocy of what we had done came into stark and frightening focus. We were building an aquarium with no idea as to how to run one. We still had no idea where to find live stingrays from nor how to transport them; we didn't know how to care for a conger eel, what qualification you would need to dive with sharks, or indeed whether that was even allowed. My only relevant experience was with water treatment systems in swimming pools but the main focus there was in killing any creature in the water not keeping it alive. At the end of the final interview with the last of the potential operators we realised how exposed we were.

John Parkes turned to Giles and me and asked, "Can you two run this place?"

"Certainly," we replied……. after all how difficult could it be?

CHAPTER 23　　　　　　　　　　　　　　　　　AUTUMN 2000

AQUARISTS ASSEMBLE!

"You know you're an Aquarist when you cry at the end of Jaws! "
Katy Rigby, Curator, The Deep

For an all too brief few days everything went well.

It was never easy to get the media to run a good news story about Hull and to date The Deep had had a very low profile when set against the other Millennium Projects. To be honest we rather resented this as by now we were beginning to suspect that we might actually have something quite special. So when Yorkshire TV phoned to ask if they could come and do a 2-minute update on progress for a local news programme I wasn't entirely surprised to hear myself say no. I told them that we were in discussion with the BBC about doing a documentary on The Deep, and that we didn't want to spoil the chances of this coming off. ITV sounded surprised but asked that, should the BBC pull out, I let them know. I told them I would.

I left it a week and phoned them back.

Of course the BBC had never asked about doing a programme on us but I felt they should have done, so it wasn't really a lie! Yorkshire TV later agreed to do a series of three 30-minute documentaries which were aired nationally during our pre- opening.

The Business Centre was also progressing on time and to budget. During the planning stage of the project the Business Centre had been the solution to both our revenue and our earlier capital problems, but since then and with the complexities of planning for The Deep, it had never really had the attention it warranted. Luckily, under the eagle-like stare of Freya Cross, our newly appointed Business Centre manager, it had been progressing quietly throughout the last year and would clearly soon be ready for handover.

We had now turned our attention to the promise we had made to the Board that we would operate The Deep. Whilst we had paid for a lot of expert advice on aquarium operation over the years I had suspected that we had always been speaking to the businessmen behind the aquariums, not the guys who actually look after the fish. Indeed up until now the advice about actual fish had been pretty thin on the ground, as evidenced by the difficulty we had had in obtaining a species list. Of course by now we were well known to all of the aquarium operators in the UK as potential competition and so we could not reasonably expect them to help us recruit our own staff, particularly, as given the size of the industry, we would be targeting their own people! Without their help where would you advertise for a head aquarist? *Fish Keepers' Weekly*? In the end I decided to write personally to the head aquarist of each major UK aquarium, asking that if it were within their corporate policies they circulate the enclosed advert to any one they think may be interested. Of course those who were interested replied themselves, and we ended up with a strong shortlist. None stronger it transpired than Dr Dave Gibson.

Dave Gibson was in that great tradition of The Deep, the right person at the right time. His diving credentials, so important to being able to operate safely, were impeccable as were his academic qualifications and his experience of working as senior Curator for Phil Crane's brace of facilities. Just as important for us was to discover that his own personal beliefs on issues such as animal welfare, environmental sustainability and the role of education in aquariums were so close to our own. Like so many of the staff we were eventually to recruit into our Aquarist team he had, wanted to work for a charity where they felt that their own beliefs would be less compromised by the realities of commerce.

Dave asked for two things at interview: firstly that he would be allowed to carry on attending various regular conferences and that secondly that he would never be asked to do anything which he felt jeopardized his team's safety. We were delighted to agree. As soon as he arrived I showed him round and gave him a simple brief: get me the fish by opening and keep them alive and healthy.

Dave seemed impressed with our efforts to date until he asked to see the quarantine facilities. We explained that we had none and asked if this was after all entirely necessary. Dave explained as patiently as he could that whilst many of the animals we would get would come from other aquariums and even fish farms some animals would come straight from the Ocean and would carry many forms of diseases and parasites, and that if these were introduced into a closed system like ours these would in all probability spread to all of our fish within weeks. So yes, if we didn't want to be replacing stock every few months a quarantine facility would be good. Not to mention the fact that it would be a fundamental prerequisite for a Zoo license. "What Zoo license?" I asked. I could see Dave suddenly realised the size of the task he had. It was one of those Sea Badger moments, but at least now we were hearing the questions we needed to address.

Dave soon started to recruit his team of aquarists, and not before time, the main tank was already beginning to take shape. At this stage, before the acrylic windows were fitted we could walk straight into the tank at ground level. Even as rough concrete the space was awesome. Over 30 feet tall and capable of holding 2.8 million litres of water and 87 tonnes of sea salt, it felt more like the inside of a cathedral than a fish tank.

Dave was quickly joined by the first of his team, Katy Rigby, Graham Hill and a few months later by Andrew McCloud and Richard Oades. Conscious that few Hull residents would be able to compete for these, the sexiest of all the jobs we had to offer, we advertised for a trainee aquarist and asked for no more than a love of marine biology. We received over 600 applications and ended up recruiting two Hull youngsters, one male and one female, Kirsten. Kirsten remains with us still after over 10 years as do Katy, Graham, Andrew and Richard.

We were soon into the pre-Christmas period of 2000, and Santa had been Ho-Ho-Hoing and wobbling his clinically obese belly since early autumn. The shops were filled with stressed-out housewives grasping at the last box of dates which, while they were destined to grow blue green fur and be binned in March, were none the less vital if it was to be a "proper "Christmas. The building's complex steel skeleton was in place and the majority of the contracts let. Whilst we were still some fifteen months from opening, we began to feel that we could by now at least have some confidence in the final estimated out-turn cost. In agreeing to manage The Deep ourselves I had by implication committed to a much more long-term position; my task was no longer about delivering a building and then stepping aside, it was now about opening The Deep and operating it into the future. It was time to really commit, and so after an entire career in the embrace of Local Government, I left and became Chief Executive of The Deep and a full-time employee of EMIH. As such my first task was to get some reassurances that our over-spend (or under funding) was still manageable, by which I meant between £2 and £3 million, and so I eagerly awaited my first regular budget update as Chief Executive from the project's Quantity

Surveyors. The fact that the project's Quantity Surveyor had asked to present it to me in person was I thought very professional, he was clearly aware that as The Deep's new boss, I would need to understand the budget in some detail.

I was looking forward to the meeting. Carefully allocating limited funds in order to maximize the impact the attraction would have to the visitor was a task I relished, a little less on floor finishes would mean a little more could be spent on landscaping, and I still had a few late improvements to the displays which we might consider if we could only close the funding gap. Dave Gibson was busy scouring the vicinity for suitable sites for a quarantine set up and so I invited just Neil and Giles to join me. The meeting began with Keith German and the Quantity Surveyor handing out copies of the monthly report. I was familiar with these, and had a growing collection of them next to my desk, charting the ebbs and flows of the costs. There was, as always, only one figure worth looking at, the estimated final out-turn figure. Once this was noted, the discussion would no doubt focus on any significant changes during the four weeks since the last report, and conclude with a discussion as to what actions should be taken. We all flicked through the thirteen pages of the report to the final page and stared! Neil began furiously flicking back through the report, page after page. I assumed I had missed a page, and began blowing and thumbing at the edge of the final page to separate it from the apparently missing page 14. "It's not good news, I'm afraid," said Keith, helpfully. "As you can see the gap has risen to £6 million " It was actually £6.1 million, and I can remember wondering when it had been that £100,000 that we didn't have had become so insignificant that it now merely qualified as a rounding off figure? Keith continued, "We have factored in all the problems we know about and tried to make sensible assumptions about claims etc." The discussion that followed went through most of the stages of mourning, shock, denial, anger... having tried these all on for size we collectively opted to stick with denial! After all, this was probably a worst case scenario; perhaps additional claims wouldn't materialize, or could be fought. Perhaps if the budget could move up by £3 million in 4 weeks it could move down by the same amount. I knew I could only go back to our funders once more, and to do so I would need accurate figures. Nothing would look worse than asking for help to fill a £6 million gap only to find out in another four weeks' time that it was in fact only £5 million. I asked Keith to look again at the figures, to justify every overspend, to look for economies that could be made. We would deal with the problem after Christmas. Who knows - the New Year might bring us some of the Luck, which, in the past, had always arrived just when we needed it?

CHAPTER 24   WINTER 2000/2001

IN THE BLEAK MIDWINTER

"Lack of money is not an obstacle, lack of an idea is an obstacle."
Ken Hakuta

The Lucky Little Devil hadn't been paying attention; instead he had treated himself to a long Christmas break in Lapland. Truth be told, he was moon-lighting as one of Santa's little helpers and although viewed by many of his fellow workers as an unwelcome economic migrant, a sponger and accused of taking advantage of the good wages and free Elf care that went with the job, he was, at least by his own standards, working hard. Until that is the January layoffs began and Santa's Personnel Dept. discovered that the Lucky Devil hadn't given his real name on his application form. Rumours began to be heard about how Devils by their nature were an untrustworthy ethnic minority and as this spread to the rest of an already insecure workforce, stories and comments began to be heard as to how this Satanic Little Helper was stealing not only the jobs that no self-respecting Elf would do, but were now even moving into the Magic Cobbler market, traditionally controlled by the Elfish shoe cartel. The trouble really kicked off though when the Lucky Devil was seen with a very popular and young (by Elfish standards) dance partner. Although closely related to Elves, the Lucky Devil's foreign accent and the fact that he was, so to speak, naturally lucky with girls, always made him popular with the ladies. In one of Lapland's famous Lap- dancing clubs the Lucky Devil was soon regaling her with tales of how he had this very important job to get back to in the aquarium field.

Ironically it was the gnome behind the bar (who of course should have known better given their history) who spotted the illicit clinch and started the name calling but when the fight broke out it was the Lucky Devil who finished it with lucky punch after lucky punch. Still when the institutionally racist Elf Police arrived the LLD's luck finally ran out. Beaten and stitched up tighter than a kipper in a safe deposit box, the Lucky Devil was thrown into a cell. As he sat in the corner he began to get the feeling that he was meant to be doing something important, something to do with fish, something ......Oh shit , ...Yes indeed little Lucky Devil, as you say, Oh shit!

During Christmas I had just about begun to come to terms with a £6 million gap. If, for the sake of argument, the new figures showed it was in fact only £5 million, then I felt confident that we could trim say £1 million from those contracts which we had yet to let, then our gap would be only £4 million and this still included £2 million of contingencies which we may not actually spend. What's more, we could lease a lot of equipment spreading the costs over subsequent years, and we still had other funding options including a private foundation called the Garfield Weston Foundation, to explore. Given a fair wind, therefore, it was possible to convince myself that we probably didn't have a funding gap at all. Thus insulated in the blue asbestos comfort blanket of self-delusion I drifted through the festive period and awaited the next, and I hoped more accurate, budget report.

Neil, Giles and the others gathered as before in what we laughingly described as our Board room. By now our Quantity Surveyor had developed a sort of black humour about the whole project. He was close to retirement and had that devil-may-care attitude which often comes from impending financial security. I noted that this time he had brought no written report to distract us. He crossed his legs and casually brushed some dust from his knee.

"You know we said it might not be a gap of £6 million?" I nodded sagely, all that worry, and I was about to be told that I had been right not to panic. "Well", he continued "we were right, it's £9 million!" We all sat open-mouthed. Taking our silence as a queue to continue, he went on. "We also did what you asked and reran the construction programme and you can't finish the building, and have it opened, by the end of 2001 as planned"

Neil, whose face had already been through fifty shades of Grey from the first news, turned several shades paler still. He spoke softly, slowly emphasizing every word. "Colin, if we don't finish by the 31st of December 2001 then we lose the European grants, that's £7 million!" Now it was Giles turn to blanch and speak: "Colin, if we lose the European grants the Millennium Commission won't be able to match them, it's written in law. They can't give us any money which isn't matched by others. We will lose another £7 million. " Even in such circumstances I could still do simple mental arithmetic, 9+7+7=23. We were now £23 million short, with fifteen months until opening.

By coincidence we had already spent about £23 million on the project. To cancel it now, whilst not impossible, would probably also require all of this to be repaid. I had been Chief Executive for about six weeks and I had lost an additional £20 million. At this rate I was in danger of making Nick Leeson look frugal.

To the layman, it seems incredible that the costs of projects can run away like they do. Certainly people can understand how there may be the odd unforeseen consequence, event or even catastrophe which may cost a bit more than expected but it now appears to happen so often, particularly with big public projects that ,to many, it looks like it is being done deliberately simply to get the project agreed. The astute reader will by now have realised that I am cynical enough to agree, sometimes it is in everyone's interest (everyone, that is except the paying public) to at least, let's say, take an optimistic view of costs in order to get the funds agreed and contracts signed. Certainly if you ask a signature architect to build you an icon, you shouldn't be surprised if sometimes costs come second to quality. Having said that, in our case the seed of the problem was there from the start, written with the best of intentions into the initial agreements with our funders. Firstly, the Millennium Commission felt that it was not unreasonable, given that the Millennium was somewhat of a fixed point on the calendar, that all of its major projects should be completed by 31st January 2001 and being in the final round this gave us less time than we really needed. Add to that a client who had never built a project before and which was distracted by the need to still raise a significant proportion of the money and we already had a potentially explosive mix. When the initial work to pull the design team together took longer than hoped and the architect had had a number of abortive attempts to come up with a design we were happy with, then the mix became a ticking time bomb. In order to be able to deliver The Deep by the deadline, we had had to enter a contract whereby the detail designs were developed at the same time as the building was going up. Like a teacher who only needs to keep one chapter ahead of her pupils this was fine as long as the designs arrived, correct first time and on time. On time that is in order to allow for the materials to be sourced and delivered, time for them to be damaged en route, lost, or to be the wrong size, colour, or to fail to get custom clearance in Taiwan. Time enough to have the right staff on site from the right sub-contractors with the right skills, training, documentation, attitude and tools to put them together in the right combination and all this of course also assumes that there will be no changes which require the whole lot to be torn up and moved six inches to the left! So to recap, a virgin client was building an incredibly complex aquarium whilst not, as yet, being in possession of the full designs (or as we have seen, the money!). Even given all of this we could at least have had a better grip on the problem if only our Quantity Surveyor had been more central to the process. Indeed I had proposed at the outset that he should base himself in the architect's office in order to advise as the designs were developed, but this was greeted with a sharp intake of breath by all concerned followed by a dismissive put-down to the effect that the experts knew what they were doing and it would probably be best if I were not to embarrass myself by making such suggestions out loud in future.

Without being privy to the decisions as they were being made the Q.S. was like someone trying to keep score in a football match by listening to the roar of the crowd!

So it was that the design had failed to come together as we had hoped and the builder had had to stand men down waiting on a drawing. It only needed one link in this daisy chain to break and another day was lost, and another claim would soon follow.

In building projects, time really does equal money so keeping on programme had been key. After some earlier delays I had instigated a weekly review at which we would go through progress in detail with the Project Manager. Every week it had been the same story. Progress was slow but we were told we were not yet behind schedule. By compressing the work programme we were told we could still deliver The Deep on time. Week after week the programme would become more problematic as it was squeezed tighter and tighter together, until like a coiled spring it would pop out and we would be told it was now impossible to complete on time. In the weeks in which this happened the project programme could go back as much as two months. It had felt like we were going backwards and now the costs had proved that feeling was right. Now the reality had been laid bare, all the delays the redesigns the complexities had all crystallised into one number: £23 million.

The scale and seriousness of the problem had suddenly all become blindingly obvious. Even though the Millennium Commission had long since reinterpreted the date of the Millennium as being the end of 2001 we were still behind programme and now we were £23 million short.

After speaking to David Gemmell, we agreed to call an emergency Board meeting for the following afternoon, and, as much as I wasn't looking forward to it, I also knew that the sooner one can share such news with others the better. Even with my limited grasp of bankruptcy law I felt it prudent to invite our lawyers and accountants to the meeting. The Board's reaction to my news was as unexpected as it was welcome.

Whilst by no means dismissive of the problems we faced there was no hint of blame, only a business like determination to address them. They expressed confidence in my team and my ability to work through the issues and completely failed to panic. As the meeting drew to a close it was suggested that we all go for a drink in the local, one by one the Board members came to put their arm round my shoulder and give me a few words of support. Whilst each of the Board members were successful business men or academics and therefore bought great knowledge and skills to the venture, I doubt if anything they ever did on the project was as crucial as sharing those few hours with me before I drove home for what promised to be a less than relaxing week-end.

By now I knew the symptoms of stress, at least the everyday common or garden variety of stress, and for that matter so did my family, sleepless nights ,loss of appetite , short temper , but that night my body moved into completely unknown territory. Lying in bed, more out of habit than any reasonable expectation of sleep, I began to shake uncontrollably. My heart raced in my chest. I sweated as if it were a balmy summer's evening not a freezing mid-January night. I thought that on top of everything else I was going down with flu, the perfect end to my week from Hell. Next morning I managed to get a rare Saturday appointment with my doctor who told me what I had already guessed. It had been a panic attack, not good but not terminal. After stopping off at home to arrange some additional life insurance, I took the family to Princes Quay Shopping Centre. Feeling even more reluctant than usual to take much interest in wandering around New Look with my wife and girls I wandered off alone. Mike Killoran caught me staring into space and with his normal enthusiasm whisked me away for a coffee. He was so positive that I could not help but feel better; illogical as it was, he still believed in the project and in me. He accepted that this was a temporary setback but simply refused to be defeated by it.

Evolution has given us two defensive strategies whenever danger threatens: either we can run or we can fight .Of course the key to survival is choosing the right one! A three foot tall, sloping fore-headed homo erectus is not a coward for choosing to climb a tree and lob coconuts at a 300lb Sabre Toothed Tiger. Neither is he brave if, when he finds himself cornered by said Tiger, he picks up a pointy stick and yells in the Tiger's face. The reality of the situation dictates what needs to be done. In our situation running or hiding from the Tiger would not have helped, since eventually he would catch me. My, indeed our, only option was to come out fighting. We had to find in our team the enthusiasm, the energy, the guile and the intelligence to find £23 million in less than 500 days. I called Neil and Giles into my office and set about the task; as soon as we began the weight seemed to lessen. We were doing something, we were still fighting and we felt better for doing so.

Clearly the key to this situation was the programme. If we could resolve that, then the European grants and their Millennium Commission match would be released and we would be back to a gap of £9 million. Having little confidence in the consultant's ability to hasten the work, we agreed that Neil should try and establish what our funders considered a "finished " building. Would it need to be open to the public? Have its roof on or what?

Whilst we waited for an answer we asked ourselves who else had an interest in us succeeding. Not simply who would benefit from our success, but who could not afford for us to fail. The answer was obvious: if we went bankrupt the Council may well have to pay back the funds already spent. It had acted as guarantor on a number of our grant applications making it responsible for seeing that the project was delivered. Secondly, the Millennium Commission: they had been monitoring the project since the beginning and had no more spotted this situation than we had. Also, they could ill afford an embarrassing skeleton of a building being left to rot in Hull. In both cases there was no option which would not involve either the Council or the Millennium Commission in more costs. The truth was that the price of ensuring our success would be less than bringing about our failure; we just had to make them see that! Despite this logic, we knew that to go to either the Commission or the Council with a naked request for additional funding would meet with a resounding no! Before we did so, we would need to take a long, hard look at where we and others had gone wrong and take some tough decisions to ensure that, if nothing else, the situation didn't get worse. We had to be able to identify what had gone wrong and we had to be prepared to take more than our share of the blame.

We would need a cunning plan. One which made it clear that we accept full responsibility for the problems we faced, which set out the actions needed to put right the historical problems we had uncovered and which shared the financial pain equitably. Of course if either the Council or the Commission refused to help, the other would be both less willing to help and less able to do so, and so we would have to take both partners along in parallel.

What's more time was running out. It would surely only be a matter of days before the contactors on site started to ask questions as to our ability to pay and if we couldn't convince them we could, the site might simply close down. If work on site were to stop the financial and reputational costs of restarting it from scratch would in itself mean a complete meltdown. This meant that not only did we need two yeses, but we needed two quick yeses.

Amongst all this I was in no position to give Freya any meaningful support with the Business Centre, and she was left to carry the whole burden of the final handover and snagging alone. It was a burden she carried with an uncomplaining stoicism. On 12th February 2001, Freya was handed the keys to the completed Business Centre and with them we were handed our first good news in weeks. The Business Centre, built as it had been to a much more conventional model, had been finished on time and on budget. They were a stunning set of offices, particularly the southern anchor unit which boasted a floor-to-ceiling window over the Humber.

We needed to be on site now monitoring progress and costs and so we began to plan that, as soon as the snagging was completed, we would decant the team, Neil, Giles, Louise, Diane, Linda and a few others from our damp, drafty and cold offices on Ferensway into our own top quality branded offices.

But for now we needed to concentrate on our financial plans and so Giles, Neil and I met again to discuss a way forward. We had to try and find a way through this which would ensure the support of all the players. Neil had by then had it confirmed that our European grants were not at risk unless the money itself had not been spent. This meant that, barring significant further delay, this money and its equivalent amount from the Millennium Commission was, as they say on the game shows, safe.

Neil would have to ensure that we drew European grants down as quickly as was allowable but suddenly our gap was back to a mere £9 million. We started with what **we** needed to do, and top of this list was to acknowledge our own lack of construction expertise, and to recruit someone to deal with the design team on our behalf.

Secondly, we could not go forward without offering a significant saving, and so after a quick but realistic review of contracts such as tank dressing, graphics, landscaping etc. we agreed that we could reasonably undertake to save £1 million from the contracts still not let.

It is amazing how quickly even Government agencies can react when necessary and, whilst there was no short-cutting the process, we soon had an indication from

Government Office for Yorkshire and the Humber that if we could increase our outputs, more jobs mainly, then a further half a million might be possible from them. We had always been conservative in regards to the number of jobs The Deep would create and so we felt this was to achievable.

We also knew that other Millennium Projects such as Eden, Magna and others had been strongly advised to make use of a complex leasing arrangement but we were also aware that such schemes were becoming increasingly problematic and it had been a route and an added complication which we had hoped to avoid. Nevertheless we could no longer afford such luxuries and we felt sure that the Millenniums Commission would insist that we pursue the idea. We would have to find a partner bank but if we could navigate the process we would liberate perhaps as much as £3.5 million.

To date the Council had not been a major funder having provided only about 5% of the cash needed. Perhaps we could ask them for £1.7 million and then get the Millennium Commission to match this.

There were a lot of ifs but it was a plan which would reduce the gap to just £500,000 and so that would be our target to raise from sponsorships and other charitable trusts. That then was our basic plan, but there was a big difference between a plan and a solution - if we were to turn the former into the latter we would need our Lucky Devil like never before.

CHAPTER 25

SPRING 2001

THE LUCKY DEVIL Vs. THE MILLENNIUM BUG

"We must believe in Luck. How else can we explain the success of those we don't like?"

Jean Cocteau

Back in Lapland the Lucky Little Devil had of course been unable rather than unwilling to give his real name to the police, which had done little to endear him to the authorities. Eventually he had pleaded that it was against his human rights not to be allowed some contact with the outside world, and despite the blindingly obvious flaw in his argument he had convinced the Governor and had finally been given some privileges in his Lapland prison cell.

Chief amongst these were his laptop. Discovering the joys of the internet, he had just gone on line and was surfing the net. He had found an adult chat room for similar minded mythical beings and was currently composing a rather obscene e-mail to his old girlfriend, the Millennium Bug. The Lucky Devil was convinced that he had caught a virus from her during their last exchange and was about to compose a particularly vicious accusation to her when he hesitated.

The Millennium Bug was actually much better looking than her name implied; indeed she had tried to change it by deed poll to Y2K which she thought sounded more feminine, like a perfume. Indeed some thought her if not beautiful, then certainly fascinating and many of the Lucky Devil's friends had become obsessed with her last year and had spent fortunes preparing for that special date, which for some reason or another she never actually arrived for. The Luck y Devil's monitor screen jumped and a message came through. "Hi big boy, you still working on that fishy thingy or will you have time for me when you get out?" It was signed Y2K. Y2K, thought the Lucky Little Devil, what a good idea - if I can't have my own name until I finish with The Deep I can at least have a cooler one than Lucky Little Devil. He began to type. "Hi Y2K, what's up? 2LD". Yes, he thought that looked better. Before pushing the send button he clicked his mouse again to check everything was indeed still fine with The Deep. "They must be nearly finished by now", thought 2LD.

His screen went blood red, a large white warning sign flashed incessantly, a range of gauges were hitting danger level. Programme at critical, budget in chaos, morale lower than a snake's belly and the Board as nervous as a group of very small nuns at a penguin shoot! "Oops!" he thought; it was time to get back to work and quickly.

The Lucky Little Devil guessed the combination on his cell door and found himself in a party of Elfish prison inspectors, he picked up a spare clip board and by repeating words like" Interesting" and "I see" every few minutes he soon found himself being given a simple buffet lunch and waved off the premises by the Governor. "Why didn't I think of that before", thought the Lucky Little Devil...

Whilst we had been keeping the Millennium Commission up to date (we had no choice as they were routinely copied in on our monthly budget reports), it was now time to see them face to face. Mike O'Connor was the head of the Commission and was not unreasonably sick to death of having to take the public criticism every time a Commission project went over time, over budget or failed to attract the visitor numbers promised by their sponsors. He had taken it in the neck for the Dome, and had been hung out to dry by the politicians who, having been hands on during its formative stages had now distanced themselves from the project faster than Lewis Hamilton on speed. The Commission was admittedly a major funder of many of the projects with problems but they were never the only funder and were in any event not the project's builders, project managers, Quantity surveyors or originators. Yet it was Mike who had to answer to the media every time there was a real or perceived problem. He was even blamed for the failure of the Leeds Armouries and other similar projects even though many had had nothing to do with the Millennium Commission.

He was not going to be the most receptive of audiences for our tale, but our case officers who knew us better than Mike were definitely more understanding. They felt that we had been let down and that we were at least displaying the appetite and abilities to sort the problem. Even when things had been going well we had always made a point of sharing everything with our funders, we had always been open with them and had, we like to think, treated them with the respect someone deserves if they trust you with their money. Now this trust stood us in good stead.

Mike was as expected less than sympathetic, but he listened to our story and our plan. He agreed to consider our request for help.

Whilst we waited for the Commission we went back to the Council and explained the position. I have no doubt that, having left the Council only weeks earlier, I was able to gain access and to be heard in a more positive atmosphere than might otherwise have been the case, and so with David Gemmell again by my side we met the senior Councillors again. We explained to them that the reality was that they had underwritten every grant we had received to date. If we failed to build what we had agreed to, it was the Council that would have to repay all of the money so far spent. We explained that we were in no position to borrow money from elsewhere as even if we could afford to one day pay it back we were an untried organisation with no trading record or credibility in the market. In short my pitch to the Council was that no one else would be stupid enough to give us any money, so would they!

To be fair the Council had gotten away lightly so far, and apart from gifting the land which, given its crust of pollution, had questionable value anyway its entire cash contribution to the project had been around £2 million, still good value for a £35million asset.

Our plan to use any contribution from the Council to unlock an additional grant from the Millennium Commission was welcomed as an equitable and realistic way of resolving the problem and we left the meeting feeling that at last perhaps our luck was beginning to change. The plan was beginning to fall into place.

Things were now moving quickly and the Commission came back with their response to our request. They would help but they had some demands. Firstly, they wanted to see evidence that we could achieve the £1 million savings target we had set ourselves. Secondly, they wanted the Board to appoint two new members from the private sector. Thirdly, they wanted us to appoint our own construction expert to act as client interface with the contractors, and finally, as we had suspected, they insisted that we pursue, with them, a leasing deal which would have the effect of helping to close the capital shortfall.

All in all this was great news, and we felt ourselves take another small step away from the brink which would have left a half-finished aquarium rotting slowly back into the mud of Sammy's Point.

With only a year or so until we were due to open and with new budget pressures still appearing, we needed our construction expert now! Luckily, Robert Haskins from

Government Office in Leeds felt he knew just the man, and recommended John Dixon to us. John was a white-haired sixty something from the tough part of the Welsh valleys, he was relatively short in the same way Napoleon was! He had had a lifetime in the construction industry and not only knew most of the tricks but had clearly written the instruction book on many of them. John had worked on a number of Millennium Projects, most recently at Magna and now hot-footed it down the M62 to take over the construction process from me, and not a day too soon.

I introduced John to the design and construction team and closed the door on them. I had this sudden vision of myself as a big plump pigeon having escaped from the claws of the neighbourhood cats and instead introduced them to my new friend the Rottweiler. The days of my worrying about the construction largely ended that day. Now it was time for the consultants, designers and builders to start worrying.

It's difficult even now with hindsight for me to identify what was the essential change John made. Certainly he seemed to speak the same language as the construction team, by which I mean Anglo-Saxon. Perhaps it was simply that we now had an individual whose expertise was in construction. Whatever it was he had, he had lots of it, and now all I had to worry about was finding the rest of the money, and running the thing!

One of John's first tasks was to oversee the installation of the large acrylic windows. Acrylic is preferred to glass in aquariums, firstly because it is stronger than glass and is better able to withstand the pressures involved with keeping back almost three thousand tonnes of water, but also for the fact that acrylic is absolutely transparent, unlike even the best glass. The largest panels weigh several tonnes and have to be manoeuvred into position with great accuracy. Under normal operating conditions the weight of the water pushes the windows against their silicon sealant stopping any leaks but until the tanks were full they have to be pushed outwards with large braces. Any slip and the panel would need replacing and, given our precarious finances, the delay in manufacturing and shipping such specialist pieces would this late on have been disastrous. The panels were lifted into position and sealed without a hitch. For what felt like the first time in months a major construction landmark had passed according to plan.

Whist we had a name for our project we could not describe to anyone what it was in less than about 800 words. This was in danger of making the posters a bit unwieldy and the leaflets the size of *War and Peace*. We had to find a descriptor, a word, a phrase which at the same time communicated what The Deep was and to some extent what it wasn't. Until now we had a wholly unsatisfactory phrase of "The Deep, a World Ocean Discovery Centre". Whilst we felt this was clumsy we finally dismissed it after carrying out some modest research with local school children. It would appear that kids are at least two steps ahead of most marketing managers. They equated Discovery Centre with a museum or library which in their eyes were perhaps two of the most unattractive places for a fun day out. I was reminded of a presentation I heard from the Chief Executive of the Imperial War Museum where she began by pointing out that one of the problems they face is that their title includes three of the least fashionable words in the English language, imperial, war and museum. I didn't want to make the same mistake.

So if The Deep wasn't going to be a "World Ocean Discovery Centre", what was it?

At the suggestion of our Millennium Commission case officer, we employed a company with specialist experience in the marketing of visitor attractions and after the obligatory two day brainstorming they presented to us their proposal: "The Deep, the Aquarium of the Future". Now even to a layman like me that seemed to provide us with two problems. Firstly, once again we were back to the A-word; if The Deep was Hull's aquarium, that's all it would ever be. To be frank, as an aquarium, The Deep was never going to be that big; the plans as they were at that stage included only a dozen tanks and yet over 100 audiovisual and interactive displays. Even if the A-word worked initially to attract customers, we were bound to receive complaints if this was our major selling point.

Secondly, of course, the problem with being the aquarium of the future is that it is only a valid title until someone else builds another aquarium. When that happens, you automatically become the aquarium of the past and despite our galleries on the history of the ocean, that didn't seem a particularly inviting prospect from a marketing point of view.

This was an issue we had come back to time and time again and was beginning to feel like the problem we had had with The Deep Theatre. It wouldn't compromise the opening but it would make marketing The Deep tough.
Perhaps, like The Deep Theatre, it would need alcohol to resolve it!

CHAPTER 26

SUMMER 2001

THE PM

"It's a visitor attraction then."

Tony Blair

We moved our offices from the cold dampness of Ferensway into our very own hi-tech Business Centre and immediately began to feel that being on site would help focus our minds on progress. It needed to as we were now entering the end game. In the next 6 to 9 months we would either resolve the problems we had or the project would fail to open, or perhaps worse still would open with crippling debts. Although time wasn't on our side, I took comfort in believing that the closer the building came to completion the less likelihood there was that more unforeseen problems would crop up.

The Business Centre had attracted its first few tenants, and the site was now tidy enough for us to plan for its official opening. With our ongoing budget crises, we would need all the friends we could get in London and so we asked Judith Donovan, a Commissioner and one of our most staunch supporters, to be guest of Honour. More out of politeness than in any expectation that he would be able to attend, we also invited John Prescott our local MP and Deputy Prime Minister. As our launch day approached, Freya and I were busy arranging catering, invitation lists as well as a short film presentation for our VIP guests, when David Gemmell, called. He had received his second call from the Deputy Prime Minister about The Deep, but this time in happier circumstances. John had told him that Parliament was breaking up that week and that Tony Blair would be in Hull on the day of our opening, helping John to celebrate 25 years in politics. John asked if we would like the Prime Minister to open the Business Centre for us. In these early days of his premiership Tony Blair was popular in a way that other politicians could only dream of. He was a British Kennedy, but with more conventional bedroom habits. We said yes and immediately, began to change all of our plans.

Even before 9/11, the security for a Prime Minister's visit was significant, and what with the searches, the protocols and the various egos of our other guests to be considered, I suddenly found myself having to introduce Tony Blair without having prepared anything to say. As he entered the room I immediately understood what those remarks about him having charisma meant. Behind him was the Deputy Prime Minister, the Minister for Sport and Hull's other rising political star, Alan Johnson, who later became Minister for Education, Home Secretary and Shadow Chancellor. As Tony Blair and I stood waiting for the short introduction film to end, he glanced out of the window and asked about The Deep: "What is it? " Once again my inability to speak in the presence of important people took over. I quickly tried to recall all those discussions I had had about how best to describe The Deep. All those branding workshops, where we had asked, "If The Deep was a person, who would it be?" "If you were trapped in a lift with the Queen and had 15 seconds to describe it, how would you do it?" When the moment came I still had no answer. "It tells the story of the world's oceans", I began," It's a cross between a museum and an aquarium, it uses a variety of interactives to explore the oceans through time and depth." He looked at me bored, "It's a visitor attraction then". "Yes", I replied sheepishly, "Yes, it's a visitor attraction...."   In a few seconds I would be standing on the raised platform introducing Tony Blair and I still had no idea what to say. I needed some serious inspiration or some luck.

At the back of the room the Lucky Little Devil arrived, picked up a glass of wine and pushed through the sea of well-trousered legs present and whispered in my ear…

"Ladies and Gentlemen, it's a great testament to Hull's progress towards becoming a new Tourism Destination that the Prime Minister, the Deputy Prime Minister and two other ministers should all choose to start their Summer Holidays in our City. You're all very welcome."

"You know there are three things I've always wanted to say in my life, the first is to be in New York and say 'Follow that car'. The second is to be stroking a white cat, to spin in my chair and say 'ah, Mr Bond, I've been expecting you'. But the third, I get to say now: 'Ladies and Gentlemen, I'd like to introduce the Prime Minister.' The Lucky Little Devil's suggestion went down well with the audience and the PM, and that night we joined him (along with about 200 others) for a Chinese meal in John's favorite Chinese restaurant in Hull. When eventually John Prescott left he thanked us for organizing the event that afternoon and offered to help if we ever needed it. The event had suddenly shot us up the Millennium Commission's credibility table. Mike O' Connor who had been present had chatted to the Prime Minister and for once had been congratulated on a project.

Early the following week David Gemmell, John Dixon and I visited the workshops of Scenic Route. The exhibitionary itself was being manufactured by them in York which meant that we could easily visit to review progress. Whilst on paper the exhibition looked strong, seeing it come to life, as a team of expert model makers, artists and craftsmen did their stuff was a revelation. The fossil wall which had originally been conceived as a relatively small piece by MET Studios was now to stretch from one end of the first gallery to the other. Our vision for it as a section of rock face which had collapsed revealing an array of marine fossils had worked well. We had shown the fossils in their raw state and in three dimensions rather than the rather sterile, picture gallery way which was the tradition. Scenic Route's workshop was the size of a small aircraft hangar and everywhere we looked plaster was being mixed, fibre glass sculpted and plastic poured. Our guide was Colin Pyrah, the MD of Scenic Route. Near the end of our visit he led us through a curtain of plastic sheets and into a small paintshop. Inside a man sat crouched over our model of the sea bed adding textured paint to a model of the world some 3m by 2m. This was to be the introductory piece. The idea had come from our visit to Lisbon but had been developed by us into an atlas without sea. In Monterey we had decided that it should form part of the introduction, and now here it was. Colin spoke apologetically," I'm sorry we are having some difficulty modelling parts of the sea bed". I looked a little closer and could see his point. Large areas of the sea bed were flat and featureless," Oh no, Colin, this won't do!" I began, "We want the ocean floor modelled to show there are mountains and valleys under the sea". Colin looked disappointed that I was displeased. "I understand we need to do better, but the problem we have is that only about 10% of the sea bed has actually been surveyed". Even John Dixon felt this was not an unreasonable excuse, and so we told Colin to do the best he could. It did, though, illustrate how much we all still have to learn about the two thirds of our planet which is covered in water.

Whilst the plan to close the funding gap had progressed well, we were still almost £4 million short. The plan showed that this would come either from the leasing deal the Commission had been encouraging us to pursue or from other smaller grants. Without the leasing deal in particular though we would still run out of money before the building was finished.

The problem was finding a bank prepared to take the risk associated with partnering a new untried and to date unprofitable organisation. The key was for our financial advisers to find us a friendly bank. As Dave Gibson was working 14 hour days to equip his newly acquired offsite quarantine facility, to source and prepare for his fishy friends to arrive, so Neil was working just as hard trying to push through a deal with a bank. One by one the well-known banks pulled out. The bank that likes to say yes said no. The world's local bank didn't operate in Hull and the one that likes to give a little extra gave us nothing whilst the Black Horse got spooked and galloped off into the sunset. As the search widened, first to European banks and then worldwide, we were left with one last bank still interested in helping us, The National Australia Bank.

As the deal inched forward in their London office all looked to be going well. They received the standard reassurances from ourselves, from Government Office and from the Commission and we cleared the deal with the Charity Commission. The deal was now almost complete; we had spent a small fortune on financial advisers to get it this far but all that would be worthwhile as long as the NAB could get a final sanction from their head office in Melbourne, which should - we were told - be a formality.

By now John Dixon had the design team and builders in a vice-like grip that made their collective eyes water. He knew the details of every contract, he knew every milestone on the programme and he knew immediately when things weren't happening. In achieving this he had used some revolutionary and highly complex management techniques. In short he got off his arse and found out. Whereas I had been told that the building site was technically the property of the builder until handover, and therefore avoided site visits unless absolutely necessary, John would sign in and be on site every day checking progress, quality and, where necessary, even managing individual workers. Of course this ruffled some highly paid feathers but the trouble was that John was almost always right. His standard riposte was therefore that if they had been doing their jobs properly he wouldn't have to interfere. On costs he would argue over every penny. If there was any doubt as to who was to blame he would argue, bully and negotiate until he was happy we had a fair deal. Meanwhile BDP were stepping up to the challenge set by John and now had a small team working alongside him on the project. As the Summer began, they were busy gaining all the permissions necessary to build the new footbridge across the river Hull, a process that was long and complex, but which boiled down to ensuring that, not unreasonably, any structure built in the river should not interfere with the navigable channel.

As soon as these permissions were in place the first few piles were placed in the river and the world exploded!

The river users reacted with fury to the positioning of the piles, and the press quickly and comprehensively ran with the story. The river users felt that transporting thousands of gallons of highly explosive fuel oil in and out of a narrow river in notoriously difficult currents and in what was a busy city centre was difficult enough without having the river width reduced by a third. Whilst I thought they had a point, I was reassured by our consultants that we had carried out all of the necessary consultations, we had all the permissions in place and so, as non-experts in maritime navigation, we felt we should push on. I checked once more with BDP that we did indeed have all the permissions and decided that we should explain the reality of the situation to the river users. It was not an easy meeting, and at the end we could only agree to differ. The bridge-building would continue in the river even if not between the protagonists.

Dave Gibson had identified a building for a quarantine facility and after completely reviewing the species list he began to source the animals. From his contacts at Blue Planet he was able to get our two Nurse sharks which had grown too large for their home. Dave had removed the Brown sharks from the species list as unsuitable for captivity and instead found two Sand Tigers in Florida. Despite their fearsome name, there is a long history of keeping Sand Tigers in aquariums and they are more predictable to handle. The shoal of Golden Trevally was captive bred in Spain and could be shipped whenever we were ready: so, so far so good. Dave was concerned to ensure though that we only used wild caught fish from properly managed areas and from ethical sources. He explained that many Coral fish were caught by dynamiting the sea and collecting the stunned fish that float to the surface. The only reliable way to be sure that our fish were sub-adult and collected in a sustainable way was apparently for him to go to the Indian Ocean and to spend three weeks diving the reefs watching the whole process. Clearly this was a tough job but someone had to do it! Dave bravely volunteered and disappeared leaving the rest of us up to our knees in builders' dust, paperwork and a small mob of seriously disgruntled river users. As hard as I tried I could not think of a single convincing reason why I should go with him.

We continued to push further ahead with the bridge hoping that the furore would calm down; after all we had the permissions and this fact alone, almost by definition, proved we were right to continue. Worryingly though the users continued to object and despite the Council having been a consultee, they also seemed to be beginning to side with the users. To reassure myself yet again I went back to BDP...

"These river users, we **do** actually have all the permissions in place, don't we? "

"Yes, absolutely, you don't think we would have continued to build if not, do you? ", asked the young administrator. He briefly looked up from filling in some routine form, and smiled at his colleague, as if to say: does he think were stupid?

"Well, as long as we're sure"

I still felt uneasy but turned to leave. " Yes, don't worry all the permission are in place.......and then, without looking up from his paperwork added, all except the Council's, obviously."

To cut a long bridge short, a number of Council departments had been consulted on specific issues but these did not in themselves constitute "permission". Having received no objections from departments, the consultants assumed that the corporate body could not object. But with a band of extremely angry sailors warning of apocalyptic accidents that's exactly what they would do. Of course even the Council needed a reason and so the argument turned on the definition of "interfering with the navigable channel". The navigable channel is clearly marked on the charts and the bridge was well outside it. But interfering with the channel did not mean simply avoiding building in it. It appeared that manoeuvring a fifty-foot vessel in a side wind was trickier than we had thought.

The press called it a "A Bridge not Far enough", we had no choice but to accept that the whole bridge would have to be re-engineered. It was painful, late and embarrassing but it was also the right decision. Luckily with John now on our team, we would, for once, avoid being stuck with most of the additional costs.

CHAPTER 27　　　　　　　　　　　　AUTUMN 2001

BIOLOGY

"Plans are only good intentions unless they immediately degenerate into hard work."

Peter Drucker

Dave Gibson had by now returned from his trip to the Indian Ocean and was soon off again to Florida filming our three documentaries with YTV. The trip was a great success. He had sourced some of the key species and had been able to check in person that they had come from both appropriate and sustainable sources. The producers were also happy that they had some fabulous footage of Dave and Gaynor Barnes diving with sharks and we now had access to all that footage to use in the display. Now all we had to do was to make sure we actually had a display to show it in!

The main tank had received its final clean and the rock work was being applied. Soon the individual pieces of artificial corals would be placed in position and the tank filled for the first time. In order to protect the large acrylic windows from accidental damage they had all been covered in foam and so the only view we could get of how the work was progressing was to either enter the tank via a series of ladders or to peek through any tiny gap in the covering. David Gemmell and I would sneak a peek whenever we could, it was good to remind ourselves of how far we had come and see the quality of the work being carried out. We knew that the tank would have to be ready soon for its first fill as it was biology that was fast becoming the most critical part of the programme. The rock work had to be finished, only then could the tank be given its final clean and be filled with fresh water. This had to be left in order to allow any residual chemicals to leach from the rock.

Assuming no leaks, and we knew this was a big assumption, then the water would have to be flushed from the system and the tank refilled with salt water. The whole system would then have to be allowed to stand for three weeks whilst the filters built up the layer of natural bacteria which would make the system work.

All of which might sound easy until one realises that just one of our tanks held almost 3 million litres and the biggest water main provided to the building was 2 inches in diameter. Every fill would take almost 2 weeks and that wasn't factoring in the fact that when salt water was involved it all had to be mixed by hand in tiny batches, and the salt, all 87tonnes of it, would have to be taken up in the lift a bag at a time.

The main tank was filled and we waited to see if it would leak. After a few hours small drops of water accumulated at the base of all of the large windows. They gathered and formed growing pools of despair on the floor.

It was condensation!

As soon as it was clear that the tanks didn't in fact leak we managed to get partial possession from the builders and Dave Gibson and his aquarists became the first operational staff on site.

However, Dave Gibson wasn't the only one being kept busy. My management team were all about their business. Neil (apart from the high level funding issues to see through) was also dealing with ticketing machines, audit controls, financial procedures and cash-handling systems. Louise, who by now had become our Personnel Officer and to be honest the organisational brains behind the preparations for the operational phase, was recruiting everyone from guides to receptionists to caterers and car park attendants. Given the interest locally, she had chosen to recruit in a sort of X Factor audition style. Linda Martin and Susan Hornby , who were in charge of PR and marketing respectfully, were knee-deep in leaflets, artwork, brand books , marketing plans and advertising rate cards. Whilst our head of education was working on her lesson plans, Katy and Graham (our new senior aquarists) were busy with writing dive manuals, sourcing feed for the animals and choosing a project vet, as well as overseeing the commissioning of the tanks and water treatment systems.

My job was to try and spot what hadn't been done.... which, mainly thanks to Louise wasn't much. With only my experience of opening swimming pools to draw on, my philosophy was that, whilst we wouldn't be able to think of everything, nevertheless the more preparation we could do, then the more time we would have to deal with the unplanned-for bits when they did occur.

One such "unplanned-for bit" began to be whispered about as soon as we had started to take guests around the building. The cantilevered ramps which were to take guests from the start of the displays on the fourth floor to the lagoon area on the third seemed to vibrate like a rope bridge in an Indiana Jones movie whenever anyone walked down them. Were they indeed safe? To find out we would need to run additional tests which would not now be completed until days before opening. If any, even minor, problem was found we would have to cancel the opening, possibly for as much as six months whilst we carried out additional strengthening works. God knows what this would have cost and despite John's assurances that we would not be liable for any problem, experience had by now taught me that all problems end up being the client's problem.

By way of some light relief from the relentless frustration of the construction process Giles, David Gemmell and I decided to ask Dave Gibson to show us his newly arrived Golden Trevally. These were to be an important part of Dave's vision for the way the Endless Ocean tank would look. A schooling species, these fish had been sourced from an aquarium in Spain and were captive bred. The species list showed them as being approximately 1 metre long. It was my first visit in some weeks to the quarantine facility and it was clear that the aquarists had worked a minor miracle in turning a rundown old paint warehouse into what looked like a cross between a science laboratory and a brewery. Giant circular tanks fed from a network of overhead pipes which splashed and gurgled as they filled with freshly treated water. Perspex anti-gassing chambers bubbled with algal growth whilst earnest young staff carefully transferred brightly coloured liquids from test tube to beaker. It all looked very impressive. Giles asked some intelligent questions whilst the Chairman and I hopped impatiently from foot to foot eager to see some fish. We had, by now, seen the rockwork take shape in the cavernous space of the main tank and over 5000 individual models of coral placed expertly on it but it was always going to be about the fish! Eventually Dave Gibson took us to the largest of the blue circular tanks. Some 5 metres across and 2 metres deep , David and I had to be given small boxes to stand on .We peered over the edge as Dave, proudly and slowly drew back the nylon sheet that covered the top of the tank to reveal our shoal of Golden Trevally. David Gemmell looked at me with one of those looks that says "We are in big trouble, kid". Circling in the distant recesses of the tank were 50 or so tiny fish. These fish were so small that together they wouldn't have made a decent fish cake. Once inside our enormous main tank they would be more difficult to spot than the Loch Ness Monster playing hide and seek. If our customers wanted to see one of these little critters they would probably have to be prepared to camp out in front of the main tank for several weeks! Dave Gibson quickly noted our expressions. "They will grow quickly, you know" said Dave defensively.

"They'd better", said the Chairman.

Soon after that the first of the smaller sharks arrived at our Peel Street quarantine facility in their so-called shark coffins and were soon feeding well.

It was early December 2001 when I walked across the car park and was called over by the site foreman. He gave me a small bunch of keys and explained that whilst there would still be builders on site for some months that he was now handing over the rest of the building to me. And so, with less ceremony than it takes to sign for a package, the building was officially ours.

CHAPTER 28 WINTER 2001/2002

WHAT THE F*** IS A SUBMARIUM?

"When ideas fail, words come in very handy."
Johann Wolfgang Von Goethe.

We were still awaiting a final decision from the National Australia Bank over the leasing deal, without which I knew we would run out of cash within weeks.

The delay was starting to gnaw at my insides, but there was no time to dwell on it. We had to push on with the day-to-day trivia of opening as if all was well. So it was with no great enthusiasm that in December 2001 I agreed to go on a short management retreat offered by our bank, the Royal Bank of Scotland. I first agreed to go after hearing that the event was to take place in America, but after 9/11 it had been hastily rearranged to take place in what was considered to be the much safer venue of Madrid. The bank's idea was to provide managers in small and medium sized businesses with a series of one-on-one meetings with leading experts in their field. This would allow the participants to access a quality of advice which would otherwise be unavailable to them. Whilst a number of experts were taking part, my own concern was to spend some time with the marketing and PR gurus. I had still not resolved the strapline question, as my brief conversation with the Prime Minister had illustrated, and now we had run out of time, the printers were waiting.

Ironically the trip was almost cancelled at the last minute when a day before the event Madrid also suffered a terrorist attack, but in typically British style we all voted to press on mainly because we couldn't be bothered with all the paperwork involved in cancelling.

One by one my fellow participants had their hour's consultation with the marketing experts and one by one had come out beaming and enthusing about how they intended to sell their sausages on the Internet or to franchise their corner shop across China. When my turn eventually came I wearily laid out the problem as I had done so often in the past. I showed these experts the video of the building and exhibitions and explained the problem. The question really was quite simple, what is it?

Whilst they were genuinely taken aback by the building, the displays and the concept, they too had no idea of how to describe it. As my hour's consultation ground to a close I smugly rose, collected my papers and said "Don't feel bad, guys. We have been working on this for five years, I am not surprised that you have failed". Luckily, they took this as a personal challenge. "Wait, we have some spare time after dinner tonight, we will get together then. You are not leaving Madrid until we solve this problem." I looked around at my surroundings for a moment, one of the best five-star hotels in the centre of Madrid. I thought of all the problems waiting for me back in Hull and agreed to stay. Later that evening we began yet another conventional brain-storming session. Liberally lubricated with Spanish beer, we ended up with every wall of the room covered with sheets from flip charts but still no solutions. Having exhausted almost every combination of the words museum, discovery, attraction, ocean and several dozen others, I decided to call it a night. I rose from what was by then something of a drunken stupour and announced that this task was impossible, we would never come up with a word that described The Deep because such a word simply did not exist. As I turned and staggered towards the door, an equally slurred and inebriated, suspiciously pixie-like voice behind me said, "Well then, let's make one up!" I turned, "Can you do that, can you make up a word?" We looked at each other, someone must make words up, and someone must have made up the word aquarium. Invigorated we ordered more beer and tried again.

The Deep was certainly part aquarium but was also part museum and part vivarium, even part planetarium, so the final bit seemed easy. We then asked ourselves what was unique about The Deep, what set it apart from conventional aquariums and it was clearly depth. Both physical depth, but also intellectual depth, we would look at the subject deeper than most. And so words like subterranean, subway, submarine gave us the prefix and the word Submarium was born.

The next morning we asked the rest of our colleagues attending the event, would they rather go to the aquarium of the future or to the world's only submarium? The result was unanimous. They wanted to visit the world's only submarium. When we reminded them that they didn't know what a submarium was, the most common reply was: "Yes, but if you've got the only one, I want to come and see what it is".

In the days and weeks that followed we defined a submarium as a visitor attraction which tells the complete story of the world's oceans and so when, during the opening week, a reporter from the Telegraph phoned and asked for such a definition, we were ready. What we were not ready for was his reply, which was, that he "thought he remembered that's what a submarium was, he just wanted to make sure that no one had made the word up"!

I returned to Hull later that same day and after a brief report to the Board, The Deep at last had an answer to the question, what is it?

Within days the slogan was being splashed onto leaflets, balloons, banners and web sites, The Deep, The World's only Submarium.

Whilst by now we had full possession of the building, the building works themselves were far from finished. A final programme which had been due to finish in 30 days' time was still running 8 weeks late. Despite this no one was yet willing to give us a guaranteed finish date but we could wait no longer, we had publicity to plan and distribute, advertising to book, staff to train and a hundred other things which needed a final decision on when we would open.

Aware of the slippages we had seen in the programme in the past we had always chosen our words carefully when answering press enquiries about a firm date for opening. We had been saying for some while now that we would open in spring 2002, hoping that we could make the February half term, but despite a newly acquired sense of urgency on site it was clear that the programme was now so compressed that this too was an impossible target. This left Easter as the next sensible target date, traditionally the busiest time of the year for attractions.

We decided that the time was right to put the builders under the pressure of working to a public deadline and announced the opening date as Saturday 23rd March 2002.

Not surprisingly our builders were reluctant to agree a date, but John took them into a padded room and they soon emerged expressing their boundless joy at the prospect of an Easter opening.

Dave Gibson was most affected by the delays. Every day that went by without us having full access to the building had meant less time for him to commission the water treatment systems and acclimatise the fish. The main tank was the biggest concern. Most aquariums keep their sharks away from the smaller fish (for obvious reasons) but we had always intended to have a more realistic open ocean display. The aim was to try and show that sharks were not psychopathic killing machines, the fishy equivalent of Hannibal Lector, but that like other predators part of a wider ecosystem. The secret to doing so was to ensure that they were adequately fed, a task which our emerging team of aquarists accomplished by training the sharks to expect food at regular times and to associate being fed with strong visual clues.

Secondly it was felt important to introduce the various species into the main tank in a very particular order. This would allow the smaller fish to establish territories in the tank and to find the quiet, protected spaces which had been designed into the rockwork for just this reason. Unlike many of the tasks we still had to complete we couldn't speed up this process by throwing resources at it. Biology wouldn't wait and it wouldn't be rushed.

Within days and with our quarantine facility at Peel Street at full capacity and unable to hold everything much longer we moved the first, smaller fish into their new home.

The Golden Trevally had, as Dave had promised, grown considerably but the entire shoal was still able to hide behind a modest size rock. Elsewhere in the building the café was being fitted, the education rooms equipped and the reception desk built but it was Scenic Route (now Paragon) who had the fun jobs. The fossil wall was brought across from their workshops in York in panels and transformed the first galleried space. They fitted John Czarky`s graphics and built the deep sea research station in Deep Blue 1. The exhibition was literally coming to life in front of our eyes, and it just kept getting better and better.

With all the heavy equipment out of the way it was time to remove the protective coatings from the main windows and to see for the first time the tanks as the public would see them. The main tank was magical. As we had planned, its far wall wasn't visible through the column of water and you could genuinely believe you were peering into the open ocean. The rock work was fabulous. We had seen so many aquariums where the rock looked exactly what it was, carved cement, but this had been sprayed on and as a result it looked random and intricate. But it was the corals which set the whole thing off. They had been taken from moulds of real corals and coloured with a rich palate of hues. Luckily we had spotted that whilst water filters out the red spectrum very quickly (which is what makes the Ocean a deeper blue as you descend) this doesn't happen over 10 metres and we had been concerned that our deepest tank would look exactly like out shallowest lagoon tank. It was a risk, as it had never been done before, but we had asked that the manufacturers reduce the amount of red dye in the corals as they go deeper in our tank. This had worked perfectly, and subtly gave an impression of even greater depth.

The corals seemed to pulse with life as the sapphire blue light shone in shafts and danced outside the tank and around our heads as if we were standing within the ocean itself. Yet this was still only the background, the real attractions, the sharks, had yet to be introduced, then it would really come alive.

We couldn't wait to see the larger animals in their new home, literally, for as nature restricted our time at one end so protocol restricted it at the other end. A planned opening day of the 23rd March would mean a Royal opening on the 22nd, and a VIP Opening on the 21st, a partners' opening on the 20th, a press preview day on the 19th and a tour for hairdressers and taxi-drivers on the 18th. (After all who is it that talks to more people in a day than these, and whose support would we need to win hearts and minds in the community?) Add these together and we would have to have the last of the fish in a full week before we were actually due to open.

By now we were fast becoming an operating company rather than a development one, and in most cases we were feeling more comfortable because of it. Whilst the construction process was not past giving us the odd scare, John Dixon's presence at least meant that we were able to deal with them better. Of course with every detail of the building that was finished we felt more and more confident that the major budget crises of the past few years were behind us. For Giles though it was time for him to make a decision; there was never really a role for a deputy Chief Executive and Giles could not easily see himself in an operational role. Despite the fresh culture that David Drewry had brought to the University, Giles did not want to return to his old administrative role in academia either, so when an opportunity arose to take an important role in establishing the University's new medical school Giles left the project. He had been the unsung hero of the early years. His intelligence and hard work were great assets for us. His pedantry had, on the other hand, sometimes been a frustration to those of us who do not choose our words with the precision and skill of a diamond cutter. When faced with the huge number of practical, urgent, decisions that we now needed to make I'm ashamed to say that not having Giles pointing out the flaws in whatever course we took was a bit of a relief. For all that the City of Hull and I owe Giles a lot.

Neil Porteus has a special expression he adopts to impart bad news. It was a look that I had long been able to recognise at a glance. I steeled myself, then as he entered my office. "I've just been on to our advisers, they say there's a problem with the leasing deal, and it's the same one we've seen with other banks. Basically the Head of NAB's London office is still concerned about our credibility and without something more he feels he will have a problem recommending to his Board in Australia to go ahead."

It was the news I had been dreading.

"The thing is," Neil continued, "This is a really small deal for them and because it's small they need convincing that we have some gravitas. This proposal is going to their Board in Australia in the morning, now that's a rubber stamping exercise, they will go with London's recommendation, but at the moment London is thinking of pulling out."

"Can we buy some time, postpone the decision for a few days until we can get something together to convince them?" I asked.

"We can't delay, all the paperwork has been drawn up with this date in mind, so it's now or never."

The lack of progress on this deal should have warned us that all was not well, but there was little we could have done. There were no other banks left to approach even if we did have the time. The consequences of failing to find a partner, even now just weeks before our opening were immense. We had been relying on the funds that a leasing deal would provide to pay our outstanding bills and we had no other lines of credit established. Even assuming that someone would agree to give us a loan we had no realistic way of repaying it.

We were building a tourist attraction in one of the least fashionable cities in the UK. The experts were predicting that we would attract around 220,000 visitors in our first year and with these numbers we could survive but not service a loan of £3 or £4 million.

If the deal didn't go through, then we would still have to pay the team of advisors, and those fees equated to close to another £1 million. With such a debt, our future was about as rosy as the serving wench in a vampire movie, it was inevitable: The Deep would bleed to death.

But if there was one thing we had learned in the last few years it was that the universe rewards action. We wouldn't shrug and accept defeat after going through so much. We decided that it was time to use our nuclear option, and call in John Prescott's offer of help. We would ask John Prescott to speak to the bank's President, simply to let him know that The Deep was important, that we were a reputable organisation and that our aims were supported by Government.

We had been rescued by fate, providence or Luck so often that we began to believe all we needed to do was to do our best and that Luck would see us through. This felt like the last time we would need him, but I wondered if this time Luck would be enough - after all it wasn't so much luck that we required as a miracle and we needed it right now.

Firstly we had to keep the ball in play so the first thing was to get a message to the bank telling them to expect a call from the Deputy Prime Minister. Using John's local constituency office I managed to get his Westminster office number and phoned. His secretary explained that, whilst she was sure the Deputy Prime Minister would be willing to help, he was at present out of the country at a Commonwealth conference in New Zealand. According to his itinerary he would be asleep at present and was flying out first thing in the morning, ironically to Australia. She would try to get a message to him but could say no more than that. In desperation I managed to get through to Alan Johnson's office. Alan promised to fax a letter giving both his and John's support, a copy of which we received within the hour. It was great of Alan to help but at this time he was not as senior as he later became, and we didn't know if it would be enough.

The next morning (the morning of the Bank's meeting) I thought I might try one last move. I would phone NAB, and ask if John had called. If they at least believed that given more time I could have enlisted John's support that might be enough. After all anything was worth trying.

I was quickly put through, and I began to explain that John was in Australia. The Head of NAB interrupted my flow, "Yes, I know, he spoke to me at home late last night from the plane, he spoke very highly of The Deep. I feel sure we can now recommend that Melbourne goes ahead".

Was this our mythical little helper, or a side of national politicians we never hear much about in the press? I don't know, but once again it showed how so often little bits of luck like phones working and like bankers not being at the theatre can change the course of events.

The next day we heard back from the Garfield Weston Foundation, a Charitable trust which we had applied to some months earlier. I remember writing to them that in delivering something like The Deep in Hull we felt that we had almost climbed Everest and that we were now just metres from the summit. We weren't asking them for a hand-out… but a hand-up.

They sent us a cheque for £250,000 and with this our funding gap which had stood at over £23 million just months earlier was finally closed. We would open as David Gemmell had always promised with no debt.

CHAPTER 29   SPRING 2002

THE OPENING

"Where so many hours have been spent in convincing myself that I am right, is there not some reason to fear I may be wrong?"
   Jane Austen

With this, the Lucky Little Devil had just about completed his task and was now looking forward to receiving his secret name. When the post finally arrived he was somewhat disappointed that his long-awaited letter came in a plain manila envelope. He opened it slowly with all the dread of a set of hospital test results.

> Dear Candidate Lucky Devil,
>
> Congratulations on completing your task to grade…C+…, (The C+, had been written in hand and in green ink.)
> We are therefore pleased to enclose your secret name (which for security reasons can be revealed by scratching the box below with a coin). We hope your name brings you much happiness.
>
> Yours faithfully,
>
> The Dept. of Mythical Creatures.

The Lucky Little Devil grabbed a coin and scratched at the box below, Slowly his name became clear……R….RO…RON…."Ron", said the Lucky Devil, out loud, Yes, I could be a Ron……" C…RONC…."That works less well", he thought … CHRONIC…."That would be harsh"……SYNCHRONICITY! "Synchronicity", thought the Lucky Devil, "sounds a bit like a bad folk band but I could make that work". He posed for a moment in front of a mirror, "Hello, I'm Synchronicity, I made The Deep happen."

With only days to go before the big day we heard that the structural tests on the walkway ramps had given us the all clear. With this last construction issue out of the way and with our finances fixed we were finally able to turn our full attention to the opening. Joining the smaller fish in the main tank were a pair of Zebra Sharks, two Sand Tigers a shoal of Jacks, White tip reef sharks , Green Moray Eels, large groupers and half a dozen wonderfully named Sweetlips. A final clean and we were ready for our first visitors.

One of the first groups to get a preview of The Deep were the staff and their families. The reaction was, of course extremely positive but I was acutely aware that they were all our guests or our staff, and that I couldn't necessarily read too much into their enthusiasm.

At the end of the evening Lisa my daughter who by now was 14 came up to me and simply said "Well done, Dad". It was the nicest thing she had said to me in two years, indeed it was one of the only things she had said to me in two years. But of all the compliments both deserved and not that I have received about The Deep, it is still the one that means the most.

The opening of a few of the more successful Millennium Projects had seen traffic jams clogging nearby streets on their opening days, and part of me wanted to see the same. I would fantasise about being interviewed on television in front of queues of cars all desperate to visit this fantastic new attraction that everyone was talking about. "Mr Brown, this is News at Ten, could we get a comment? The Deep's opening has caused grid lock over 20 square miles of East Yorkshire. We understand ticket touts are offering tickets at £100 each, what do you have to say to the 50,000 disappointed customers? " I feign sympathy and manage to fake an expression of sincerity, "Please bear with us we will get you all in eventually, we never imagined it would be this popular," I lied.

Of course there were also those well publicised Millennium projects that had been rather less than successful, but by now the mood of the press seemed to have shifted. There had been so many negative stories about the Millennium Dome in particular that this was no longer news. The Dome itself had just closed, in any event. We wondered if the press might be ready for a good Millennium story. We hoped that the fact that Hull was still considered by the London press as about as fashionable as tank tops might make even a modest success a story worth reporting.

As the final days ticked down and the big day approached the media interest in the project suddenly took off like a cheetah on amphetamines. It began with stories about the architecture, but grew into a much wider spectrum of stories. The Times had listed The Deep as something to watch out for in 2002 along with a rising star of the music business Sheryl Crow, and then in the three weeks prior to opening, Yorkshire Television screened their documentaries which went behind the scenes and accompanied Dave Gibson on his trips to Florida and the Indian Ocean. The shows were a ratings success and were then screened on other ITV stations from Anglia to Grampian.

National BBC news carried the story of Hull's new "Submarium", as did Radio 4, BBC Worldwide Sky news and Time Magazine. Stories began to drift back to us that ex-pats had seen The Deep on the news in Australia, in Bahrain and across Europe. Our official press day, held a few days before opening, was a mad round of interviews, but added greatly to our national profile whilst our free day for taxi drivers and hair dressers from the city got that most valuable of PR, word of mouth recommendations. We began to be concerned that all this publicity risked giving people the impression that we were more than we were. Whilst we were proud of what we had done our budget was similar to Magna and the Space Science Centre in Leicester. It was only about a third that of the Eden Project, or for that matter the Earth Centre in Doncaster. As for The Dome, I think we spent less money on fish than they spent on Tipp-Ex! Indeed, Disney routinely spend more money on a single ride than we had done on the entire project, and yet this great PR had some customers expecting Blue Whales performing synchronised swimming displays against a backdrop of erupting volcanoes.

With this in my mind I decided to drive into work early on that first day. One of our contingency plans we had discussed was how we would cope if we or our key staff couldn't get through the traffic on that first morning. By leaving at 7.30 am, I could arrive by 8.00 am and hopefully still be able to fight my way through. As I neared the site, the traffic continued to flow worryingly well. Closer and closer, Clive Sullivan Way, Tower Street, and I was there. One lonely looking Reliant Robin sat alone and forlorn in the car park. I half expected to see tumbleweed blowing across the rows of empty car parking spaces. As I walked towards the main doors I could see the clock tower on Hull's City Centre Church, it had just turned 8.00 am. Outside the queue, if that is the right term for a family of three, stood huddled against the wind blowing wet and cold from Lincolnshire. "When's it open?" shouted the Dad over the gale. "10 o'clock", I replied trying to inject some excitement into my voice, "Have you been waiting long? "

"No just got here really, thought it might be busy what with it being new and all."

I smiled weakly. Dad turned to his wife," Shall we wait or shall we come back later?" " No, we might as well stay now we're here", she replied. I was touchingly grateful for her commitment; at least we would have three customers today.

Soon other staff began to arrive and I greeted them in reception. "Not many people waiting are there?" "Oh that's to be expected, it's still early", I lied. The pre-launch publicity over the last few weeks had been incredible and much more positive and wide-ranging than we had a right to expect. Later we calculated that the PR value of all of this was greater than the entire cost of the project. So there was no excuse if nobody came. As the last minute preparations continued, I would sneak brief looks outside, 8.30 am....8.45 am.......9.00 am......still our queue stretched no further than a super model's thong.

Soon it was time for me to give the final staff briefing. In tone it felt military. Everyone was trained, radios were issued, uniforms clean and pressed. Motivation wasn't a problem either, without exception the staff couldn't wait to go over the top. When I made my final remarks and wished everyone good luck, a spontaneous round of applause began. As the meeting broke up and staff made their way to their stations I half expected to see them passing hastily written notes to each other, "If I don't make it, Charlie, see my wife gets this for me", "Don't be silly mate, you hang on to it, and give it to her yourself when this lot is over".

There was little left for me to do now but wait. I made my way out onto a part of the roof where I knew I would be alone, and looked out over the City and our near deserted car park.

Visitor attractions are not like normal businesses which start with a small customer base and grow over time. Visitor attractions are like cinemas that show the same film forever! A tough enough proposition in any event, but if you can't fill the seats on opening night it doesn't bode well for your long-term survival. Out on the roof protected on three sides by giant air-handling housings, I took a few deep breaths. What on earth had we been thinking, an aquarium in Hull, a visitor attraction in one of the most deprived, unfashionable cities in the land. A place with the lowest educational standards in the country, the highest teenage pregnancy rates in Europe, a place recently voted crappiest town in England (largely, it has to be said by its own residents), a city which, according to one local wag, had so much trouble trying to get somewhere to twin with it that it ended up settling for a suicide pact with Grimsby! A place where unemployment was so high that even the job of village idiot was only part time. This is where we had chosen to build a new type of attraction, not Florida, not London, not even York, and the only evidence that it would work, I now realised, was a report done some 5 years earlier by Coopers and Lybrand accountants. A report based on a completely different proposal. If the Millennium Dome had failed in London and with a budget ten times greater than ours, if attractions like Sheffield's Popular Music Centre, like Doncaster's Earth Centre and others, were either struggling or had failed completely then what made me think The Deep would be any more successful. The truth was that we had begun to believe in our Lucky Devil or at least in The Deep's ability to survive, but this was reality, it wasn't a game and it wasn't fantasy. In those last few minutes before opening our doors for the first time, I realised that any one of the disasters which we had overcome or narrowly avoided in the story of The Deep so far would have been preferable to a completely finished, fully funded building that quite simply no one wanted to visit.

Perhaps all the problems which we had overcome were not sent to test our resolve but were warning us not to proceed? Perhaps we hadn't been persistent; perhaps we had just been stubborn.

It was ten minutes until opening and time to face the big day. I left my roof top eerie and made my way to reception. The queue had grown.

From everywhere cars began to arrive, buses drew up, families scuttled, hand in hand across the car park to join the throng. In these last ten minutes the queue grew, and grew. By the end of that first hectic day we had welcomed over 2,800 visitors, 6 of which were carrying banners protesting that we were denying God by preaching the new-fangled theory of evolution. Assuming they wouldn't be susceptible to reason I took them upstairs and showed them the Genesis quote which pacified them!

We had had to ban certain staff from volunteering to work on that first day just so that we had some fresh staff for day 2. This was just as well. Our second day saw 3,100 and a week later we had 5,000 visitors in a single day.

CHAPTER 30 SUMMER 2002 ....and on....and on...

POST-OPENING

"The secret of success is to get up early work till late, and strike oil!"
Rockefeller

In the weeks that followed the queues grew longer still, reaching for over a quarter of a mile. Local traders did in fact complain about the traffic chaos in the area. We were selling more food than P & O ferries and in our first year we were busier than London Zoo. By our first anniversary we had been visited by 850,000 people, we had made a surplus of £1.8 million and won a wall full of awards from best newcomer in the Leisure Industry to runner up in the best new Tourist attraction or initiative in the world. The Business Centre was over 90 % full and we had established the foundations of an ambitious international research programme which continues to grow in reputation and reach. Since then we have worked on the Great Barrier Reef and on the Great white sharks of South Africa. We have studied the tiniest corals of Puerto Rico to the giant Manta Rays off of Sudan. We have developed new medical treatments for fish and have pioneered new captive breeding techniques and the use of biological controls in aquariums. We even carried out the first CAT scan ever on a living shark!

We have built a £5 million pound extension and been named the UK's best Aquarium.

The underwater lift ride which we fought so hard for was recently named by *USA Today* as the best lift ride in the world beating the Empire State Building and the Eiffel tower.

Whilst claiming to be the most successful of the country's Millennium Projects can feel like getting a prize for being the tallest dwarf in the room, nevertheless it's true. We make more money than the Eden Project and do more conservation work. We even achieved David's definition of an Icon Building when in June 2006 we appeared on a Royal Mail stamp. We have in our turn supported over 1000 other local charities in one way or another and hosted over 300,000 visits by school children.

The Deep has become perhaps the most recognised symbol of Hull, appearing constantly in the press and on TV.

In a hundred TV and press interviews over the years I've been asked the question: "What was our secret?" Of course it was partly down to those things we had discussed on that original train ride back from London. A good story, an iconic building and excellent exhibits, but we also had a great team. It was a team who were often so young and inexperienced that they didn't realise that what we were doing was impossible, and not knowing that, they did it anyway.

It was also down to sheer determination, at least on David's part.

We had a knowledgeable and supportive Board and politicians willing to go the extra mile.

But you and I now know that we also had more than our fair share of luck.

In the chaos of the universe we can and must plan and strategise, we need to work hard and gather the best talent to us....but don't kid yourself you're in control. We still rely on the little twists of fate for which there can be no accounting. Whether an individual was in to take a vital call, or a train was late or a computer crashed such movements of a butterfly's wings can be the difference between heroes and knaves. We are in a universe where meaningful coincidences govern our lives. That doesn't mean that we should take a fatalistic view and let whatever will be, be. It means that we have to build teams and cultures that can change as fast as your luck does.

Rockefeller was once asked what the secret of his success was. He said it was to get up early, work till late, and strike oil.

He was right.

CHAPTER 31　　　　　　　　　　　　　　　　　　　　　ONGOING

RESEARCH AND CONSERVATION

"If the seas live so will the land."
Native American saying

We always said that The Deep needed to be more than a visitor attraction. It needed to address issues of education, regeneration, job creation and of course it needed to change the image of the City. Within this we always felt, I think, that Hull had always had an exploitative relationship with the sea. We had hoped that The Deep would play a role in establishing a new and more sustainable relationship with the oceans. To this end we operate an ambitious research and campaigning role which I thought you might like to know about!

The Oceans are in crisis. Mankind's impact on our seas through unsustainable fishing, Ocean acidification and climate change, shark finning and pollution have already seen once thriving ecosystems collapse. But we have also seen that with the right action that our Oceans are capable of recovery. We have seen an international movement to establish marine conservation zones and we are better informed than ever before about the threats our Oceans face.

Below is just a small selection of the work that The Deep has carried out over the years.

Red Sea Manta Ray Project with Equipe Cousteau

In January 2009 we launched the start of a 6-year collaborative project with Equipe Cousteau monitoring a number of pristine populations of Shark and Manta Ray in Sudan as part of the regional Red Sea Shark and Ray Management Programme. The project will focus initially on tagging and tracking work with financial support from The Deep (£20,000 per year) and staff time for field work each year.

The Deep is to date the only aquarium in the world that Equipe Cousteau has been prepared to work with.

NETGAIN-The North Sea Marine Conservation Zone Project

The Deep campaigned strongly for the establishment of Marine Protected areas around the English coast. The Government agreed and asked The Deep to lead the Board charged with delivering a consensus amongst sea users along an area of coastline from Scotland to the Thames estuary.

This project, known as Netgain, was chaired by The Deep which also part funded the process and provided facilities and management support. The final recommendations are now with Government. Together they will become the most important conservation initiative ever undertaken in our native waters.

Puerto Rico Trip SECOR

The SECOR project is a collaborative research and conservation project led by Rotterdam Zoo Aquarium and has contributors from Europe and North America. It aims to look at reducing the pressure placed on wild stocks of hard corals by perfecting the techniques required to reproduce the corals sexually.

Over recent years a number of joint research trips have been carried out to Puerto Rico in the Greater Antilles to study the spawning behaving of Acropora palmata (Elkhorn Coral), which is now listed as "threatened" under the Endangered Species Act in America and is being considered for inclusion in the Endangered Species List globally.

A team of coral biologists from numerous institutes in North America and Europe (including staff from The Deep) spent 10 days a year studying the spawning behaviour of the coral and collecting larvae which were settled in laboratory conditions before being shipped to North American institutes.

Lophelia pertusa data collection

It's not widely known that the North Sea also has corals. These white corals were the subject of a survey trip carried out as part of long-term collaboration between The Deep and the Scottish Association of Marine Science.

The 5 week trip was in conjunction with BP on board the RRS Ernest Shackleton. The mission was to collect information on the distribution of the CITES listed

Lophelia pertusa a deep -water scleractinian coral. Data gathered from this trip was provided to SAMS and formed part of their wider research project.

Great Egg Case Hunt

In support of a national campaign being run by the Shark Trust, The Deep has carried out shoreline surveys on seven beaches from Whitby on the North Yorkshire Coast to Mablethorpe on the Lincolnshire coast. The campaign aims to establish the presence of different species of skate and ray around the UK coastline by identifying egg cases washed up on the shoreline. This will give an indication of the relative health of the wild populations of these species around our coastline.

ORCA Cetacean surveys

In conjunction with Organisation Cetacean (ORCA), staff from The Deep spent five separate weekends on board Fjord Line ferries on the Newcastle to Bergen run surveying for cetacean species in the Northern North Sea. This is the first comprehensive survey of cetaceans in this area of the North Sea using shipboard observers and will help provide invaluable information on the effects that commercial shipping and oil exploration have on wild populations of large cetaceans in this area.

Financial support for the MCS Green Turtle tagging programme in Sri Lanka

The Deep provided funds to purchase satellite tags in support of the Marine Conservation Society's project to tag Green Sea Turtles in Sri Lanka. The tags provided important data on the lives and migration habits of these iconic animals.

Sustainable Lobster Fisheries

The Deep has provided tank space for survivorship trials in conjunction with the North East Sea Fisheries Committee project to achieve Marine Stewardship Council accreditation for the Lobster Fishery on the Yorkshire and Lincolnshire coast.

Beach Cleans

Since opening in 2002 staff of The Deep have carried out twice yearly beach cleans as part of the Marine Conservation Society's Adopt a Beach campaign.

BIAZA Reserve – Atlantic Rainforest of Brazil

The Deep sponsors a ranger in the Atlantic Rainforest Nature Reserve. This project (in conjunction with the World Land Trust) aims to conserve and protect the rainforests, land and wildlife as well as providing employment to the local community.

"Don't let it end like this.... tell them I said something."
Pancho Villa

List of plates.
1. Sir Terry Farrell's original concept, and the first design launched in early 1999.
2. The site.
3. The design moves on.
4. David Gemmell OBE, signs the Millennium agreement with Mike O Connor. With Mike Killoran and Jack Brignall MBE looking on.
5. The design develops in response to the budget crises.
6. Work gets under way.
7. The point in late 2000.
8. The acrylic tube for the lift ride is hoisted into position.
9. Inside the big tank. Jan 2001
10. I fail to explain the project to the P.M.!
11. The 7m x 3m acrylic windows are gently placed in position. May 2001
12. The Deep appears from behind its scaffolding. August 2001
13. The protective cover is removed and we get our first view of the main tank. Dec.2001
14. The (almost) finished building. Dec 2001
15. Our first resident.
16. The point, March 2002.

Notes Dec 2016

1) Amazingly improvised process –
   eg. question?! made up partners,
   france available – user competition

2) Difficulty of stabilising concept until v. close
   to the end – Sibarium ! Deep Sea

3) Amazing pick n' mix of existing
   attractions – visits, ideas, testing!

4) Separation of the university + visitor
   attraction
   eg such at gl's in book not the uni.

5) (sure of cost of energy) → 24°C?
   check was that maintainable in
   building – if no heating or cooling – mass

6) Feels sharks + polar bears so they
   do NOT eat fish
   of Penguin poster – energy + time!

7) Increase of ideas – complexity!

8) Goal / Distinctiveness
   + learning